Hearing God's Call

Hearing God's Call

WAYS OF DISCERNMENT
FOR LAITY AND CLERGY

Ben Campbell Johnson

WILLIAM B. EERDMANS PUBLISHING COMPANY
GRAND RAPIDS, MICHIGAN / CAMBRIDGE, U.K.

© 2002 Wm. B. Eerdmans Publishing Co.
All rights reserved

Wm. B. Eerdmans Publishing Co.
255 Jefferson Ave. S.E., Grand Rapids, Michigan 49503 /
P.O. Box 163, Cambridge CB3 9PU U.K.
www.eerdmans.com

Printed in the United States of America

07 06 05 04 03 02   7 6 5 4 3 2 1

Library of Congress Cataloging-in-Publication Data

Johnson, Ben Campbell.
Hearing God's call: ways of discernment for laity and clergy /
Ben Campbell Johnson.
p.   cm.
Includes bibliographical references (p.   ) and index.
ISBN 0-8028-3961-4 (pbk.: alk. paper)
1. Christian life.   Discernment (Christian theology)
3. God — Will.   I. Title.

BV4509.5.J63   2002
248.4 dc21

2002029499

Dedicated to those persons who told me
their stories of call
and
to the following persons,
who read this manuscript and
made many helpful suggestions:

Ted Bayley
Phil Branson
Bettie Graves
Don and Joan Beerline
Frances Dille
Andrew Dreitcer
Charlotte Keller
James Holderness

Contents

Preface

God has always called human beings to share in the divine mission in the world — and he still does. God calls women and men to ordained ministry in the church, and he calls other followers of Christ to special ministries both in the church and outside it.

One of the persistent questions in the minds of both serious clergy and seeking laity can be stated simply: "Is God calling me to do this work or this ministry?" A call from God has the power of a conviction that it is not our work alone but is something both intended and empowered by God.

Following closely on the heels of this question is another question of equal urgency: "How do I know the call comes from God and not my own unconscious longings or fears or even cultural influences on my perceptions and decision-making?" This question leads us straight to the issue of discernment. In this instance, discernment is the process of determining what is God's call to us and what is not.

As we enter a new era for the church brought about by swift cultural changes, the matters of call and discernment are now even more urgent for laity and clergy. I believe the issues in this century will be especially focused on laymen and laywomen who hear God calling them to significant ministries both within and beyond the bounds of their local congregation. Some of these ministries will be callings to works of compassion, and others will be callings to serve God as a lawyer or a teacher or a construction worker. Of course God calls certain individuals to ordained ministry within the church. But increasingly I'm meeting men and women in every corner of this nation who are sensing God's call to ministries that don't require ordination in the formal sense. Some have responded eagerly and are now actively engaged in their calling. Others have not yet understood the ways of God with them and have been left wondering about their inexplicable experiences. Still others have heard the call of God but have resisted it. These various situations again point to the importance and necessity of discernment.

But laity is not alone in the need for discernment. Clergy are also feeling the pressure to test their call, to reaffirm it in new forms of ministry in a changing social context. Some of these ministers are close to retirement, but they know the context of ministry has changed. They find themselves caught between loyalty to their traditional modes of ministry and the need to respond to fresh demands created by cultural shifts.

Another class of clergy chose the ministerial profession because it challenged them intellectually, offered them a way to serve people, and gave them standing in the community. Suddenly these culturally conditioned ministers have awakened to a secular society that no longer knows or trusts the essential affirmations of the church. In short, they find themselves in a missionary situation without the skills to do basic missionary work. How do these individuals discern God's call?

Perhaps the most disillusioned group of ministers consists of those who have graduated from mainline seminaries in the last decade. Their background and experience defined ministry for them. Their training prepared them for ministry in a church of another era. Their pain can be felt in their plaintive confession: "We feel like we've been prepared to pastor churches that no longer exist." What is God's call to them?

In an era characterized by dramatic cultural changes, new demands are being placed upon ministry, and its style must change. All utilitarian and survival tactics are doomed to failure. This radical new day demands new kinds of ministry through people who are empowered by a call from God.

BEN CAMPBELL JOHNSON

CHAPTER ONE

God Is Calling Today

Hearing God's call bestows an honor unequaled upon human beings. This incomparable beckoning raises us to our true dignity as creatures made in the image and likeness of God. Ponder for a moment the priceless gift of the Creator and Sustainer of the universe speaking to you. What affirmation could be greater than the awareness that God knows your name, speaks to you, and invites your participation in the divine intention for the world? This divine call to ordinary people like you and me has been occurring from the very beginning of the Christian movement — and it still occurs today. I'm encountering — in an unprecedented way — numerous individuals who are wondering about God's call in their lives. Many experience remarkable signs of God's presence. And God isn't just calling people to join the clergy. His call is much broader and deeper than that. A description of a few of these calls will give you a clearer idea of what I mean.

Stories of God's Call

Richard's Story

The first person I want to introduce to you is Richard, a young lawyer about forty years old. He thought God might be calling him to ordained ministry, and to explore this call he was visiting Columbia Theological Seminary, where I taught. The admissions department at the seminary often sent me prospective students who had had a profound spiritual experience. The admissions secretary made an appointment for me to talk with Richard. When I went to my office for the appointment, I asked my administrative assistant, who is also my wife, if she knew anything about this man. She told me she didn't.

When Richard arrived, we introduced ourselves, shook hands, and took a seat at the round table I used as a desk. I asked Richard to tell me about himself and what had brought him to the seminary. He began by telling me about the mission trip he had taken to Mexico. Every day he worked with poor people to build a church, and every evening he worshipped with them. The experience had affected him in ways he couldn't describe, like a mysterious encounter with the Presence from the land of silence. After returning home, he told me, he continued to think about his time in Mexico and also began to have strange experiences — at least, they were strange to him.

At this point he paused, looked deeply into my eyes, and said, "I think I can trust you."

I nodded.

Then he continued, "He's been talking to me!"

"Who, Richard? Who's been talking to you?"

"God."

"What is he saying to you, Richard?"

"He's been telling me that he loves me and that he has something for me to do."

From what Richard had told me about his encounter with God in Mexico, this turn of events didn't surprise me. God was at work in his life.

After Richard spoke for an hour about how God was working through him in the small southern town he lived in, I shocked myself by saying, "Richard, I think maybe you should go back home and keep listening for God to tell you what you are to do in your church and community." Why was I turning him away from the seminary? (My recommendation to him shocked me because he was the first person whom I had counseled *not* to come to seminary. Generally I encouraged people like Richard to come and study for a year to explore their call.)

I chose to share this meeting with Richard because his story is like that of so many people I've met or heard about. He had been a church member all his life. Then the Spirit of God began to awaken him on a deep level. People around him suggested that he go to seminary because they didn't know what else to do with a congregant who was spiritually alive and zealous for God. Of course, these fellow members had nothing but good intentions for Richard. They recognized the dramatic change in his life, and they felt they were supporting him in God's will. But it occurred to me that, although God was certainly dealing with Richard in a special way, he wasn't necessarily calling Richard to ordained ministry.

When Richard went back to his hometown, he began doing God's work in wonderful ways. He started a small prayer group. He visited with all the ministers in town and became a unifying force among them; he and his minister started sponsoring joint services with other denominations. And Richard began to consider that God might be guiding him to seek a judgeship. God had clearly called him, but he was not, at that time, called to ordained ministry.

Carol's Story

Carol, a person whom I met quite by accident, has a different story of calling. She was indeed a person who had been touched by the Spirit of God. Carol had come to Atlanta to visit her future sister-in-law. It so happened that she was a secretary at Columbia whose office was across the hall from mine, so it was convenient for Carol to drop by my office and investigate the program that I headed.

The moment I sat down to talk with Carol, I sensed something special about her. Her face was radiant. Her voice was strong and self-assured. (Maybe "God-assured" is a better term.) Immediately I wanted to know her story and how she had come to this place of spiritual aliveness.

She described herself as having been a marginal church member who didn't participate much. Then a tragedy befell her that threatened her very existence. In a voice that bespoke amazement, she described how she was held in the arms of love during her period of angst and despair. At the time, she didn't know the name of this love, but she suspected that it was the presence of God.

As her life began to rise from the ashes of pain and lostness, she found her way to a pastor who listened to her story with both sympathy and understanding. He encouraged her to believe that the darkness was passing away and a new light was beginning to break through.

Soon Carol had individuals approaching her for help. Many asked her what had happened to her. Sometimes she felt at a loss to explain the transformation she was experiencing. More than once a person asked her how she found the peace and joy that emanated from her. She found herself almost without words but frequently answered, "I pray a lot."

Long before Carol knew about God's call to her, she began inviting women to her home for discussion and prayer. Soon the women that Carol talked and prayed with began to experience the Presence in their lives. Fortunately, Carol had a pastor who understood her budding new life. Fearlessly, he asked her to begin a class at church. When she began teaching, the handful of people that first showed up quickly grew into a large group that soon outgrew the space allotted them. Not surprisingly, more and more people sought her out with questions. Soon she was leading weekend retreats for members of her church.

When I met Carol, her "explosion" of new life had been going on for several months. At the time of our initial meeting, she was pondering two questions: How could she prepare herself for the ministry she was developing, and how could she discern the new ministry into which God was calling her?

After I had talked with Carol, I mentally added her name to the growing list of people with stories like hers that I was meeting across the nation. Increasingly I sensed that God was doing something special not only with clergy but also with laypersons. I began to wonder if God was touching the lives of unsuspecting people and leading them into more fruitful forms of ministry.

Martha's Story

In California I met another equally fascinating woman named Martha who had heard the call of God to a specific ministry. She was "quasi-clergy" or "quasi-lay," depending on how you look at it. She qualified as one of those new kinds of people whom God is awakening to the truth that there's more to life than money, power, and prestige. She had enrolled in and graduated from a theological seminary but never had the intention of pastoring a church.

I made an appointment to meet her at a little corner restaurant in Pasadena. Even before our coffee arrived, I asked her to tell me about her experience of God's Spirit in her life. She began by describing her deepening interest in God and her choice to pursue that interest. She told me that she went to seminary to find out about the God who was making himself more and more evident in her life. Shortly after she enrolled in seminary, as part of her training, she enrolled in a clinical education course. She soon found herself working as an intern in a hospital.

Her supervisor placed her in a room with fifteen little girls all under the age of five. During her brief orientation she was told that each of them had been sexually abused. This revelation stunned Martha. That evening she went home and wept. And the Inner Voice would not let her rest. Night after night she wept as the faces of the children appeared before her. Something had to be done about such a deplorable situation, and God began claiming her for the task.

Martha's concern had not abated when she finished the course, so she took the budding call with her into her next practical assignment. In addition to her classroom work, she was assigned to work in a church near the UCLA campus. She talked with the church's minister about children's needs and the persistent sense she had to respond to abused children. He encouraged her to make it a matter of prayer. Martha told her husband about the conversation with the minister and about his suggestion. To gain greater clarity, she and her husband decided to take a weekend away in Santa Barbara to pray about the calling. Both of them returned from that weekend with a deepened sense of calling.

When Martha remembered the faces of those sexually abused children in the hospital, she had a vision of getting families in the church to take these children into their homes for three or four months until the children could be properly placed in foster homes. Each family who hosted a child would have another family that prayed for them and that took over child-care responsibilities for a weekend when they needed a break. After Martha discussed this vision with the minister, he gave her permission to present it to the congregation. After hearing her story, the congregation gave $7,000 to fund the dream.

Implementing this dream wasn't easy. One problem after another presented itself — problems with local officials, with church members, and with continued funding. Through it all, Martha kept saying, "God called us to do this work, and we will do it." She found that her real test came when she committed herself to the ministry in this way.

Despite its initial problems, the ministry began to succeed and received increased local attention. After a few experiments had demonstrated the feasibility of the plan, Peter Jennings of ABC News interviewed Martha, and she was able to tell her story to millions of viewers. People from around the country began to call and inquire about how they could create similar ministries in their own communities.

Do you see how this layperson who was called by God had a vision that strengthened my conviction that God is doing a new thing in our midst?

Daniel's Story

Daniel is yet another person whose story illustrates God's call. He would have frightened some pastors with his certitude about God's work in his life. For years he had been a nominal member of a mainline church in a small industrial town in the South. He was making his way up the management ladder in the family business. At the invitation of a friend he attended a dinner hosted by the Fellowship of Christian Athletes, where he heard a highly respected local coach give witness to his faith in Jesus Christ.

Although Daniel had heard Christian testimonies before, God used this particular testimony to awaken his faith. The next week he began reading the Bible in earnest. He got up early and stayed up late to search his way through Scripture. He read the entire Bible in just a few months.

The truths of the Bible began to work their way into his inner life. They began to set him free and open him to new possibilities for his life. His behavior changed. Attending church and worshipping God became priorities for him. Talking with Christian leaders and ministers both inspired his fledgling faith and guided him on his journey.

After he had been on this journey for about a year, Daniel began to sense a call to ministry. He didn't interpret this call as an invitation to study and prepare himself to pastor a church. Rather, Daniel had a vision of training other laypersons like himself in the ways and work of God. As he described his sense of call to me, he said, "I don't see clearly what God is calling me to do, but it seems that I'm being called to start a school for equipping lay men and women for ministry." He had raised his sail to catch the breeze of the Spirit.

Daniel represents scores of laypeople who need help in recognizing God's guidance. They need discernment. I hope to be of help to individuals like Daniel who are searching for God's will for their lives.

These representative stories mirror the experience of thousands of laypersons across this nation who are being called by God to be his partners in ministry. These stories vividly illustrate my thesis that God intends to call Christ's followers into significant ministry today.

As this book unfolds, I will relate the stories of other equally serious individuals whose lives God is shaping for ministry. I'll tell you about a good friend of mine in California who has sold his business, finished seminary as a layman, and is seeking God's clear call but doesn't yet know what it is. I'll tell you the story of a woman who, after years of teaching French, felt called to minister to the dying. She studied counseling and did her own clinical work in preparation for being with people during their last hours on earth. I'll also tell you about a close friend of mine who has struggled with the institutional church for years but has found himself called into a ministry to the homeless.

Stories of God's Call to Ordained Ministry

In ways both ordinary and dramatic, God still calls women and men to ordained ministry. I've heard scores of stories of people who are in the process of responding to a call to ministry within the church. Recently I spoke with Tom Rayford, a new graduate from seminary, about his call.

Tom was raised in a Christian home, and he attended church and participated in church activities for as long as he can remember. For a long time he felt rather embarrassed about the fact that he couldn't name the specific day or time that he became a Christian, but then he began to celebrate the fact that he had always been aware of God's love for him. His call didn't come from flashing lights in the sky or from a dramatic event in his life; it grew naturally out of his maturing in the faith.

Experiences like attending conferences and workshops and going on mission trips enriched and shaped him as a young man. Through these growth experiences he developed a desire to serve God with his whole life. But he never considered entering the ministry until he was a senior in college. Then, when he was home for a visit, a discerning pastor asked him if he had ever thought about going into the ministry. He quickly responded that he had not — but still, a seed was planted. And after graduating from college, he spent a year as a youth worker in a church.

All these experiences placed ordained ministry in the back of his mind but did not, for him, constitute a call. The events that led to his specific call have an aura of mystery about them. They involved a political struggle in his home church. A slate of church officers had been drawn up, and the younger generation felt excluded from the list. The church was split down the middle on this issue, and the two sides were locked in a power struggle. Since Tom was respected by both sides, the younger group asked him if they could nominate him from the floor. Tom asked for a few days to think about it, and during this time he consulted with the pastor.

As the two talked, this interim pastor, who was an older man, got choked up and quite emotional. He advised Tom not to get involved in the church's politics. But he also made a simple, direct observation that was much more important to the young graduate: "God has a plan for you in his Church." After the meeting, Tom couldn't get these words out of his mind. So he went back to the pastor and shared his experience and asked what he should do. Within two weeks Tom began a round of visiting seminaries to test his calling. Each step he took made it clearer to him that this was indeed the work of God and that he was being called to ordained ministry. He followed obediently, and he is now ordained into Christ's ministry in the church.

In Tom's story we can see the hand of God shaping a person long before he knows what various experiences mean. Tom's story also demonstrates how God works through circumstances and through others' words of wisdom in the discernment of a call. Perhaps of equal importance for us is the realization that gentle, progressive calls have the same authenticity as dramatic, charismatic calls.

Rather than multiplying narratives of God's call to clergy today, I will use a few carefully chosen examples to communicate their situation, their hunger, and their frustration as they seek to be faithful to their call. Some of the most moving words I hear from clergy come from ministers in doctoral courses, participants in conferences and retreats, and pastors in whose congregations I've labored.

A doctoral student who had been out of seminary for about five years said to me, "I feel like I've been trained to pastor a church that no longer exists." Another doctoral student was mulling over new insights he had gotten in a spirituality of ministry course. He commented to me, "If I had tried to talk with my professors in seminary about these matters, they would have thought I was crazy and unfit for ministry. But this emphasis is precisely what members of the church hunger for."

A successful minister who was participating in a serious program of continuing education asked for an appointment with me. In the privacy of my office he confessed that he had spent most of his ministry seeking to please people, increase church membership, and raise budgets. "I feel like such a failure," he told me, "because I've focused my life on the wrong things." Another pastor confessed, "I'm weary of day-to-day ministry. I often dream of taking a few interim pastorates until I can retire."

How are these confessions of the clergy to be interpreted? You could blame them or question their integrity, but I believe doing so would miss what is actually going on. These clergy are caught between a rapidly changing social situation and congregations that don't want to change. Many of them don't know what to do about their call, the church, or their ministry.

Their congregations often interpret the pain, frustration, and confusion they're experiencing as ministerial ineptness. Instead of this negative evaluation of today's ministers, I would put forward the thesis that God is calling them anew. Their pain and loss of vision, and their resulting doubt and weariness, may be the very agents of God's call. Their experiences of powerlessness in ministry are part of God's way of getting their attention to help them make the shift to God's fresh agenda for the North American church. I would encourage these ministers to pause and listen for God, to listen until they hear their call anew.

The Mystery of the Call

I conclude this exploration of call with an acknowledgment that the call always has an aura of mystery about it. A while back my wife and I took a trip to Australia. One evening, while strolling around the Sydney harbor, I noticed a series of quotations about Australia placed on markers at intervals along the water. All these quotations had been taken from the works of literary greats who have written about the "continent down under." One of the quotations in particular fired my imagination. The Australian novelist Eleanor Dark wrote, "The land lay in silence. Out of the silence came mystery, magic, and a deepening awareness of unthinking things."

These words evoked in me a feeling of mystery, the kind we sometimes experience when awakened from a dream. It is the kind of awareness that often comes when we make contact with the holy or the inexpressible. Dark must have experienced a kind of awe when she considered the greatness of her homeland. Often this kind of experience accompanies a call from God.

I myself don't write about land or mountains or seas, but I do write about contact with the holy, about the human spirit encountered by the Holy Spirit, about the Beyond that pours itself out in our midst. The feelings that Eleanor Dark writes about seem similar to those experienced by the people who have talked to me about their encounters with God. Somewhere in the background of their stories there always seemed to be a deep silence, out of which emerged mystery, marvel, and a new sensitivity to things both animate and inanimate. As I talked with numerous people from a variety of backgrounds, a sacred arc, both mysterious and wonderful, seemed to span their stories and inflect them with holiness.

No one has described this mysterious call with more succinctness and yet more depth than Carlo Carretto in his little book *Letters from the Desert*:

> God's call is mysterious; it comes in the darkness of faith. It is so fine, so subtle, that it is only with the deepest silence within us that we can hear it.
>
> And yet nothing is so decisive and overpowering for a man or woman on this earth, nothing surer or stronger.
>
> This call is uninterrupted: God is always calling us! But there are distinctive moments in this call of his, moments which leave a permanent mark on us — moments which we never forget.[1]

In all that I write about the call of God, I'm certain that my efforts will not illuminate the mystery of God's ways with us. The origin and manner of the call will remain shrouded in the "cloud of unknowing." God's call cannot be manipulated or shaped by human hands but must be obeyed without any certain knowledge about where it will lead. Therefore, its way is always dark, lighted only by a tiny flicker of faith that creates enough courage for one step at a time.

Why do we think that God always shouts? Could it be that our insensitivity so dulls our hearing that God must shout to get our atten-

---

1. Carlo Carretto, *Letters from the Desert* (Maryknoll, N.Y.: Orbis, 1972), p. xv.

tion? Once God has gotten our attention, then comes the silence, the inner stillness of the soul that attends the Voice. In its essence the Voice speaks with gentleness and softness so that we must listen intently to hear its message.

How does this subtle, gentle voice speak with such power? How does it enter our lives with such undeniable strength and turn us in new directions that precipitate choices that change us forever? Nothing else changes us so completely as the call of God. It re-orients our whole life! The call leaves within us the residue of certitude that gives us the strength to face the doubts and struggles that are bound to come our way.

Decisive!

Sure!

Strong!

Are you feeling a call? Do you wish to answer it and get the decision over with? I have news for you: This simply won't happen. You will never finish with this call! The call of God comes long before you hear it, it lingers until you name it, and then it never completely goes away. Call is continuous! God is always calling us. One distinctive, unforgettable moment comes when you answer the call. But there will be other moments that will come again and again, marking your way and giving you the assurance that the God who called still calls.

Being chosen by God and given a place in the divine mission to the world carries with it a distinction that only the called — both clergy and lay — can fully appreciate!

I hope to provide a modicum of help in the discernment of God's call that will enable all the members of the body of Christ to respond to God in new and fruitful ways for the kingdom. I aim to assist laity in their search for an authentic call to ministry, to guide those who believe themselves called to ordained ministry, and to support ministers who are seeking to discern God's calling to them in a radically changed social context.

Myra Scovel, a woman who knew something about the blowing of the Spirit in times like these, wrote the following poem. It instructs all of us who have experienced the wind of the Spirit filling our sails.

The Wind of the Spirit
Where does the wind come from, Nicodemus?
Rabbi, I do not know.
Nor can you tell where it will go.

Put yourself into the path of the wind, Nicodemus.
You will be borne along
by something greater than yourself.
You are proud of your position,
content in your security,
but you will perish in such stagnant air.

Put yourself into the path of the wind, Nicodemus.
Bright leaves will dance before you.
You will find yourself in places
you never dreamed of going;
you will be forced into situations
you have dreaded
and find them like a coming home.

You will have a power you never had before, Nicodemus.
You will be a new man.

Put yourself into the path of the wind.[2]

The key, as always, is discernment. To encourage you along the path of call, I'm including a series of exercises in discernment at the end of each chapter. I urge you to record your responses to these exercises, because doing so will provide you with data that will be helpful in your personal choices. You will also find that the practice of writing down your answers to the questions asked and following other directives for researching your call will reveal more to you. I cannot overemphasize the importance of writing as a spiritual discipline.

2. Myra Scovel, "The Wind of the Spirit," 1970.

13

Exercises in Discernment

1. What is the world like for you? Does your world make room for a God who knows you and wishes to communicate with you?
2. Describe your current idea of what a call from God would be like in your life.
3. Make a list of five Christian individuals you know who exemplify the Spirit of Christ. Which of them seem to be living with a sense of calling? If you identified their call by the life they live, what would you guess their call to be?
4. For examples of calls recorded in Scripture, see the Appendix.

CHAPTER TWO

Is God Messing with Your Life?

A friend of mine gave me the operative word for this chapter title. He was a minister struggling with his own personal demons and seeking to right his life. At a crucial juncture in his inner battle, he received a three-month sabbatical. He needed rest, renewal, a deepened sense of call, and freedom from his compulsions.

During those three months he went to monasteries and retreat centers, seeking out people who could help him. My meeting with him came on a Sunday morning at a pancake house in Atlanta, Georgia. He was fresh from a week's stay at the Monastery of the Holy Spirit in Conyers, Georgia.

When we had ordered breakfast, he turned to me and said, "I've been hard after God these three months." And God had been after him too: as he put it, "God has been messing with my life." The word "messing" in Southern-ese doesn't mean "making a mess," like tracking red clay on a white carpet, but rather suggests that God has been touching and examining this or that and even shifting a few things around. God's "messing with our lives" means that he gets our attention, challenges our priorities, and often redirects our lives. Has God been messing with your life?

I'm assuming that you've felt some movement of God's Spirit, or you wouldn't be reading about a call and ways to discern it. I've tried to make it clear that I'm writing to the person who's had some kind of experience with God and doesn't quite know what to make of it. In these pages I want to share with you what it means for God to be "messing with your life" and how you can recognize these initiatives of the Spirit. What I have to say relates to laypersons seeking a call to lay ministry, to persons discerning a call to ordained ministry, and to clergy whose sense of call needs clarification and renewal.

I'd like you to know straightaway that involvement with the Creator can really be an awesome, challenging relationship. This divine/human involvement shrinks to insignificance the "go to church, sit in the pew" mentality of the typical mainline church member. Consider how our lives are enhanced when the Creator of the universe takes note of us, enters into our consciousness, informs us about himself, and draws us into a partnership of creativity and action. God has an interest in you and in your partnering with him in the divine plan for this earth. Think about it. There's a place for you in the unfolding drama of history.

Taking the call of God seriously demands that we repudiate the notion that God no longer speaks to people. If God doesn't speak, why should we listen? But if God does speak . . .

Proponents of the divine silence believe that God spoke to Abraham and Moses and even spoke through the mouths of the prophets. They also believe that God spoke through Christ and still speaks through the New Testament, which records his words and deeds. But they stop short of expressing confidence that God addresses us in our present situation, except indirectly through Scripture. Where is their confidence in the Holy Spirit? In the contemporary presence of Christ?

I'm convinced that the God who spoke still speaks. True, God speaks through the Bible, but the Spirit of God speaks to people and calls them to kingdom work just as in the first-century church. Some of God's people, however, don't know the source of the call, nor do they know how to respond to it. If I'm overemphasizing the obvious, forgive me. The recognition of the God who still speaks marks the dividing line between a religion of history and memory and an exciting participation in the contemporary work of the Spirit.

A Contemporary Story of a Call

Sometimes when God is at work in a person's life, her countenance seems to glow. While I was working with a congregation as a scholar-in-residence, I began to notice a woman who attended various meetings I conducted. Her name was Cynthia. She radiated a contagious joy. Something about her made me feel that God was working in her life in a special way. I asked her if she would stop by my office and talk with me, and she agreed to do so.

When we finally got together, I asked her to tell me about herself. She explained that she had been raised in the church and thought of herself as a Christian. Through high school she used her vocal talent to sing in the choir. When she went away to college, however, other things became more important and more interesting to her than God. The church and God's mission in the world slipped from conscious view.

A few years after college, she began attending church again and singing in the choir. Although she felt that something was missing in her life and in her relationship with God, she kept going to church to be more acceptable in the community. Perhaps she was unconsciously seeking God. Still, she laments the fact that she appeared devout on the outside but was confused and empty on the inside.

Then a crisis came into her life that caused her to feel rather helpless. She couldn't work out the problem on her own power. In spite of her inner pain, she put up a good front and continued to pretend to have faith and to live faithfully. As she reflected on this time, she told me, "I had my life set up just the way I wanted it, except for the one problem I couldn't resolve." In other words, she was in control.

Then, very unexpectedly, she was in a car accident that almost took her life. While she was recovering from her injuries, "something" happened to her, something that she didn't control. She wasn't in charge of this transformation, and she had difficulty describing it. She used words and phrases like "overwhelmed," "overpowered," and "something that I couldn't resist." Prior to the accident she had been zealously religious on the outside — attending church, singing in the choir, putting on a Christian face — but after the accident she felt healed and whole on the inside. God became personally real to her. She was liberated and empowered by the newfound presence of the Spirit.

When I asked her to describe for me as clearly as she could what this transformative experience had done in her life, she struggled to answer, finally admitting, "I know that God is real. I feel that God loves me. But I struggle every day with my feelings of unworthiness. I don't think that I'm good enough for God to manifest himself to me in this fashion. No matter how hard I try, I'm never quite good enough."

I asked her about her prayer life, about how it had changed since the accident. "The Lord shifted it for me," she explained. "Before the accident, I journaled a lot. I often wrote numerous pages at one sitting, but an internal shift moved me away from that form of prayer.

"Instead, I started praying in the morning, chosing a specific place to pray in my home and sitting down there. I started thinking about people who might need God's love, and I thought of them in God's presence. If nothing came to me, I simply sat with God and thought about him.

"At first I felt that I was wasting time. I wasn't accomplishing anything. I wasn't producing anything. I wasn't reading long portions of Scripture like I used to; I wasn't keeping a list of things to ask God for. Sometimes I read one verse for a week, thought about it for a while, and then took my thoughts into the presence of God.

"I felt rather guilty about not praying the way I always had. At least, I felt guilty until a group of women came to our church a few weeks ago. I talked with them about my prayer life, and they told me that I was being led into contemplative prayer, a prayer of being centered in God.

"Now after I pray, I have a deep sense of God's presence that I take with me into everything that I do. God is real, so real to me. At first, when I got home at night, I tried to turn my prayer off, like I was saying to God, 'I've been with you all day, and now I need to rest.' But I've discovered that he's with me even when I rest."

Cynthia's experiences of love and prayer prepared her for her ministry, which was suggested as a new power began to manifest itself through her. Through all her years of attending church, she had sung in the choir, and on occasion she had sung solos at worship services and other special events. She confessed with regret that her singing had once been merely a performance. But since the accident and the changes that had occurred in her, she had been experiencing an energy that was communicated through her as she sang.

I invited her to be more specific if she could. She said, "The first time this happened to me was at our midnight Christmas Eve service, when I sang 'O Holy Night.' I had always loved that song, but instead of 'giving a performance' that evening, I put my heart into my singing. Something was happening between the Lord and me. An electric feeling went through me as I sang. The Spirit affected the people in my congregation — many of them were in tears. And some of them came to me after the service to tell me what had happened to them. It seemed to me that I went to another place when I sang, and as I became totally empty, I became an instrument of God." I knew what she meant. Often when the Spirit comes, there is an ecstasy in which the singer becomes one with the song, and it is accompanied by a deep sense of peace and joy.

I myself had listened to Cynthia's story with rapt attention, nodding my head, trying to take in what she was telling me. When she finished describing that first experience of being used by God, she had an urgent question for me. "What do you do," she asked, "when people tell you how wonderful you are and how deeply you touched them?" She had repeatedly told people that the effect they were experiencing wasn't something that she was producing.

In a soft, hesitant voice she tried to explain to me what other people used by God have known. She felt so absolutely certain that God had possessed her heart and voice that she couldn't accept any praise or credit for the ministry. Being praised for God's work through her presented a new challenge. How does a person who is being used by God give the credit to God without belittling herself? Cynthia was clearly struggling with this question. But she was learning to receive people's gratitude while acknowledging in her heart that they really were responding to God's working in her.

Not only did the Spirit use her voice in a new way; her piano-playing was equally inspired. The same energy that infused her voice was also in her hands as she played either the piano or the hammer dulcimer. These were natural gifts, and she had worked hard to develop them, but now they were lifted to a new level. Not only did she become more conscious of these gifts, but she also experienced the Spirit of God working through them with power and energy. People were being affected by the Spirit, which was in her in ways she hadn't experienced before.

After I had listened intently to this amazing story from a woman who was not only gifted but also attractively humble, I paused to absorb what I had heard. Having recognized the initiatives of God in drawing her back to church, working with her through a personal crisis, and using an accident to transform her life, I wondered what sense of call she had. So I asked her, "What do you think God may be calling you to do?"

"Oh," she said with a twinkle in her eyes, "I want to play music for people in the hospital and in nursing homes." She had felt this call for several months and had been looking for ways to respond to it. Just recently a door had opened in a nursing home so that she could begin her ministry. This open door confirmed her sense of call.

Additional confirmation followed. A friend of hers had asked her to visit a pottery outlet in town where local artists displayed their wares. Cynthia had neglected to respond for several weeks but decided one Saturday to go to the pottery shop before her friend checked up on her again. More awaited her there than she had anticipated.

When she got to the outlet mall, she noticed a woman entering with a harp. Cynthia followed the woman, hoping to get some help playing her own harp (another instrument in her repertoire). To her amazement, the first woman joined a second woman who also had a harp, and the two put on a performance in the mall. After listening to them play, Cynthia engaged the women in conversation, asking if they had any interest in ministering to people in nursing homes. Her knees weakened at their genuinely positive response. She described them as three people "joined in heart and soul." Other doors have begun to open for them as a trio of disciples called to minister to suffering people.

Anatomy of a Call

Cynthia's experience has special importance for our exploration of the meaning of a call because it illustrates a number of ways in which God works in a person's life. I take as a given that you sense the Spirit of God "messing around" in your life, challenging your present direction and nudging you toward new possibilities. You probably have a notion that God is doing something with you, but you may lack categories and names to give to your experiences. What I want to explore with you next are the various aspects of God's dealing with us.

I'm holding up Cynthia's experience not as normative but simply as an example of how God "messes around" in a person's life. Even though she felt like she had botched her relationship with God for a long time, she had an idea about God's will for her. This idea was clothed with powerful emotions that demanded expression. As Cynthia and I talked, it seemed to me that this set of circumstances sparked a dialogue inside her, an inner conversation that she couldn't get away from until she embraced her call and began to seek ways to pursue it. A deeper look at these aspects of her call will perhaps assist you in recognizing your call.

It Begins as an Idea

The call of God to a vocation begins as an idea in your mind, often triggered by an event — like Peter being interrupted by Jesus while washing his fishing nets, or Ananias hearing a call during his time of prayer, or Saint Paul being confronted on the road to Damascus. You begin to have a hunch that God may be calling you to a ministry.

The call may be sharp and clearly focused, or it may be soft and less focused. For example, in Cynthia's case, she received a specific call — to use her voice to minister to people in nursing homes. In a similar situation you might have a strong sense that God is calling you but remain unclear about the specific focus. Whatever its degree of clarity, the idea emerges and gets your attention. In some ways an idea is like a conception — a flood of "pre-thoughts" invades consciousness and looks for little eggs of awareness to fertilize. And perhaps only one of those pre-thoughts fertilizes an egg of consciousness and gives birth to an idea. Only when the idea has been born can it take shape and begin to grow.

Suppose God has something for you to do, like becoming an advocate for abused children. To communicate this intention to you, the Spirit begins to act in the depths of your spirit at a level beyond the range of your awareness and outside the bounds of your control. (It's something like Jesus walking along the edge of the Sea of Galilee until he comes to the place where you're washing your nets and preparing for another day's work.) By the act of the Spirit, those pre-thoughts of God's intention begin to flood your consciousness. In your awareness they connect with your love for children and evoke images in your mind that are clothed with feelings of compassion. Through this process, occurring at the speed of thought, the idea has been born and wrapped in swaddling clothes.

I use the call to advocacy for abused children to illustrate the work of the Spirit that applies to many calls. Whether the call is to be a teacher or a businessperson, an ordained minister or a lawyer, the dynamics of the birth of an idea are very much the same.

Cynthia's idea of ministering to others through her voice had its roots in her very early years. Doubtless she thought of using her voice to minister to others when she was an adolescent singing in the church choir. Even though at that time the idea was driven by the delight of performing, it was nevertheless in her mind. After the accident and the re-orientation of her life, the idea of using her voice for God reached a new level at the midnight Christmas Eve service. At that point God revealed to her how he could work through her.

This interior, Spirit-inspired activity may be accompanied by other concrete experiences in your life, like meeting others who have an interest in the ministry you're considering. Reflecting on the idea that God has birthed in your mind may clarify your focus and shorten the time you wait for the idea to mature.

The Idea Is Clothed with Images and Emotions

When an idea has formed in your mind, it immediately seeks to clothe itself with images and feelings. Your conscious mind draws from its reservoir of both positive and negative images to clothe the call. If the call has directed you toward a longed-for activity, images of fulfillment and delight will likely attach themselves to the call. Since a person like Cynthia has gifts in music, a call to provide concerts at a nursing home no doubt results in feelings of sheer delight. The delight stems from envisioning the positive results of the ministry and from the awareness of pleasing God in pursuing the ministry.

But as we all know, other images also attach themselves to these initial calls. Most of us have an abundant supply of negative images — feelings of inadequacy, inexperience, and ineptness. These negative images evoke fear. For some individuals, the very thought of a ministry to elderly persons in a nursing home unleashes a wave of fear capable of freezing the notion in its tracks. "God would never call me to that kind of work!" they insist.

But fears of inadequacy don't sweep away the call. It may well have to withstand feelings of anxiety about experience and competency. Clearly, emotions become the driving force in our engagement in ministry. Generally a tug-of-war develops. On the one side, the gentle, seductive spirit of Christ lures us toward God's intention. On the other side, our fears, inspired by who knows what, hold us back.

Clothing the call with images from our heart begins to integrate it into our lives. Until the call becomes part of us emotionally, it is nothing more than a notion in our heads that we can manipulate and control. Attaching feelings to our images incarnates the call in our flesh-and-blood story, and passion begins to drive it. The emotions, whether positive or negative, do much the same thing — they drive our call. Our feelings, our yearnings for meaning and significance, embrace the call and energize it. Because many of us have difficulty distinguishing thoughts from feelings, pay special attention to this interplay in your own struggles with a call.

The process of concretizing the call makes it personal and real. The abstract notion, which has potentiality and possibility, suddenly begins to present itself as concrete and energized by feelings. At this stage of development, the call has become specific enough for prayer and powerful enough to challenge our volition.

Cynthia had always used her gift to minister to people through music. In her case the call became more focused when God chose to engage her in the singing of "O Holy Night" on Christmas Eve. In that moment she was given a ministry in a form she had never before experienced. And even though it exhilarated her, it also frightened her. This often happens when the Spirit of God acts through us, when we become aware that something beyond us is flowing through us. The realization creates a contradiction in our awareness. How could God use a flawed person like me for his divine purposes? To have our old, negative image of ourselves so powerfully challenged can be truly frightening. But the awareness of God's purpose for us conquers our fears.

The Emotion-clothed Idea Initiates a Dialogue

When this idea that God has something for us to do enters into our consciousness, it evokes a response from us. The inward response may be something like, "I could never do that — I'm too incompetent. I have no experience." Excuses like this arise either from our sense of inadequacy or from a disguised resistance to change in our lives. Sometimes we don't want to yield to God because our priorities would be shaken up and rearranged too drastically.

As we make these excuses, the Voice of the call responds to us. God's thought remains in our awareness, persistently pressing upon our spirit, urging us to listen. For a time we may fight against the fledgling call like an untrained citizen fighting a gladiator. Or we may give up the fight and try to douse the call with forgetfulness. Yet because God has chosen us and calls each of us into a ministry, we cannot escape the persistent beckoning of his voice. Even though we may suppress the call or ignore it for years, it finds a way of re-emerging in our consciousness.

However the call unfolds, it usually involves a struggle. Many names can be given to the struggle, but always at the center lies one issue — surrender to God. The question is this: "Will I permit God to be God, or will I continue to act like I am God?"

In Cynthia's experience, this struggle took an unexpected form. The ministry of the Spirit through her was so overwhelming that it gave birth to feelings of inadequacy and inferiority. Her singing was not inadequate, and her performance was not inferior — yet *she* felt inferior. Her question was "Why did God choose me? I feel so unworthy of the Spirit's presence and of being used in this manner." Her greatest struggle lay in accepting the graciousness of God in bestowing his Spirit upon undeserving servants.

We Embrace the Call

In a sense, embracing our call is like giving birth to it, owning it and giving it a place in our lives. Accepting the call of God into our lives means responding positively to God's perceived intention for us and emerging from the struggle in peace. As I have indicated, our interior struggle with God's call may be a struggle of wills, or it may arise from our feelings of unworthiness.

In the first instance, when we perceive God's call as an interruption in the vision we have for our lives, it is likely that we will resist this call, a resistance that sets up the inner battle. Ananias, the layman in Damascus who baptized Saul, clearly heard the direction that God gave him. But it contradicted his own vision, and so he resisted the call. He didn't know about what God had been doing in Saul, about the transformation that was underway. Many of us find ourselves in this position when we hear a call. Like Ananias, who was called to baptize and commission Paul the Apostle, we can resolve the tension by seeking greater clarity about God's call and being willing to respond.

In the second instance, our inability to embrace the call arises from our feelings of inadequacy. Cynthia originally had this response, and she was still struggling with it when I talked with her. She kept asking herself and the Lord, "Why me?" The questioning stemmed not from an unwillingness to be used of the Lord but from a paralysis caused by the wonderment that God knew her, with all of her flaws, and still wanted her for his ministry.

Changing attitudes and emotions such as those displayed by Ananias is no easy matter. Feelings don't listen to reason, even when the information that reason supplies is accurate. I have found that God will deal with us on a credit plan: so much down and so much a month. When we find ourselves stymied by either self-will or low self-esteem, we can pray, "God, I give myself to you as fully as I can now. Help me give tomorrow what I cannot surrender to you today." We can't surrender what we can't surrender — that's the simple truth. But the Great Teacher and Patient Father will work with us if we turn our eyes in his direction. After we have embraced the call, we need to do one more thing: Get started!

We Take Initial Steps

When we think we've been called by God, we should be sure that we've heard God correctly. The person who is too quick to say "God has called me to this or that ministry" doesn't inspire confidence in the more mature members of the body of Christ. Many of them have heard shallow testimonies of call that never materialized. Discerning, testing, and verifying the call of God will take time, but in the long run it will save us from error and embarrassment.

If you feel you've received a call, the first move to make might be to find a trusted Christian friend and talk with him or her about the call. Discuss what you think God is saying to you. Describe how the idea came to you and how you're feeling about it. Ask your friend for honest feedback. Does your sense of call seem to be of God? Your friend might well be able to see something that has escaped you.

If the ministry to which you're being called will be representative of the church, speak with the minister or the officials of the church. You shouldn't begin a ministry that will be perceived as expressive of the whole church without first getting approval from the church. Discussing your call with the leadership of the church not only helps you to clarify it but also informs the leaders of your vision and draws their support to your ministry.

Having made these moves to clarify and legitimate your call, begin developing your strategy. Pray for guidance from God. God called you, and God will guide you. Share your vision with others and listen to those who show an interest. Watch for doors to open and walk through them. In subsequent chapters I have more to say about each of these moves to connect with others with respect to your call. For now it is sufficient to note that these initial moves will get you on the way toward fulfilling the call you've received. Perhaps the next move on your part should be to examine your personal history for evidence of God's progressive calling.

If you should miss the call or successfully resist the call for a period of time, be assured that it will not go away. A friend of mine says that in many ways our call is like the light. We don't create light; it's just there. Likewise, no matter how much we read about it, write about it, and study it, we don't create our call. It's already there. God even has a backup ready if we reject or miss the first call. We may find our call, or trip over it, or fall into it, or reject it, but, like light, it exists separate from our search. And it will continue to seek us out.

Exercises in Discernment

1. On a sheet of paper draw a vertical line. At the bottom of the line write "Birth" and at the top of the line write "Now." Think of this line as your life from birth to the present. Beginning at the "Birth" end, slowly picture the unfolding of your life. Whenever you come to a time that you thought about God's call for you, draw a hash mark across your lifeline. Beside this hash mark write a word or phrase that identifies this moment for you. Proceed through your life until you reach "Now." Include all the experiences you had — when you thought about a call, when you resisted a call, when you asked others about a call, and perhaps when you embraced a call.

2. Revisit each of the moments of call or "possible" call. Muse over each one. Think about what God was doing in that experience. Record your musings in a notebook.
3. Write a simple prayer asking for God's guidance and help with understanding his call in your life.
4. Choose a trusted friend and share the results of your personal explorations in exercises 1 and 2 above.

CHAPTER THREE

Sources of God's Call

How does God speak to us? How do we receive the call? These questions point to both the media and the mode of God's invitation to us to share in the divine purpose operative in history. In sorting out the ways of God's call, the experience of Saul of Tarsus, who met Christ on the road to Damascus, offers us a good beginning point. Soon after his conversion, he hastened off to Arabia. I imagine that he spent those three years there learning from Christ and reflecting on how the Spirit had been at work in his life before he studied with Gamaliel in Jerusalem, before he became the chief persecutor of the church, and before he encountered Christ on the road to Damascus.

Even if his reflective powers had skipped over those early years of living in a Jewish home and worshipping in the synagogue in Tarsus, thinking about the three most recent events in his life would have taken up large spans of reflective time. For example, the image of Christ that Saul saw in the face of Stephen while he was being stoned communicated to him volumes of unarticulated meaning. In Stephen's face he saw a peace and a confidence that he had sought for years. Stephen's vision of Jesus standing at the right hand of God must have moved Saul deeply. And with his final breath Stephen cried out for Christ to receive his spirit. These strong words of assurance bespoke a victory over death that keeping the law never gave Saul. What had happened to this man Stephen that enabled him to speak with such certitude?

Simply observing Stephen face death without flinching struck a fatal blow to Saul's worldview: the world was not as he had imagined it. He believed that the Messiah would come one day; he had been taught to expect this all his life. In Stephen he saw a man stoned to death for confessing that Jesus was the Messiah. Watching a man die for his faith and hearing him talking with Jesus with the confidence that Jesus heard him seriously challenged Saul's view of reality. All of us have a worldview, of course, but for many of us it is never seriously challenged. So we live as if the way we see the world is the way all people see the world, or ought to.

An even greater issue for reflection derived from Saul's encounter with the risen Christ on the road to Damascus. On his way to harass and imprison the followers of Christ, he met Christ, and he became one of those whom he had intended to incarcerate. The hunter had become the hunted and had in fact been captured. What did this mean? Who was this invisible presence that knew him so well and turned his life upside down?

The remaining experience for Saul to contemplate was the visit of Ananias. For three days Saul had groveled around in darkness, neither eating nor drinking. Without warning there was a knock at the door. A man stood there who claimed to be sent by Christ to heal and ordain him. When he stood in the presence of the persecutor, Ananias told him that he had been sent by the Christ who had appeared to Saul on the way to Damascus. We don't know how much conversation followed this first face-to-face meeting, but we do know that Ananias prayed for Saul and that Saul's sight returned. Ananias baptized him and affirmed that Christ had called him to be a missionary to the Gentiles. Saul didn't argue but instead began to witness immediately to what Christ had done in him. An amazing power flowed through him to his hearers, and many of them embraced the faith.

When he was in Arabia, Saul surely wondered why he had been chosen. He doubtless connected the Christ on the road with the Christ who sent Ananias to heal and baptize him. These experiences became the primary material for his reflection. But the contemplation of these most recent occurrences didn't obliterate the preceding years in which the Spirit of God had been at work, shaping his life for this missionary task.

Saul's response to Christ's invasion of his life provides a model for all of us. The call of Christ isn't separated from the other dimensions of our life — our history, our background, our training and experience. The call clothes itself with images and emotions drawn from our deep pool of memory. Few of us may have the leisure to take three years to go to Arabia or Hawaii or the Swiss Alps to reflect on God's call, but we can set aside time to reflect on the call from the breadth of our personal history. Perhaps we can imagine Saul reflecting on his life, seeking the meaning of several cataclysmic events. But how does this process of reflection help us with the practice of discernment today?

A Contemporary Saul

Pablo is the fictitious name that I'll give to this friend of mine who also is struggling with his call. I first met Pablo at a brunch with him and his pastor at a hotel on the West Coast. I was scheduled to spend a month teaching and consulting in his congregation. He had been appointed chair of the committee that was planning for my visit. Pablo was in his mid-fifties and balding. At first he was quiet, listening and getting his bearings.

As the conversation continued, he and his minister and I got more comfortable with each other. I began to notice the insight Pablo had; I recognized that he was both a seeker and a doer. His manner of relating to people and the style he employed to get his ideas across bespoke a man with vast experience and finely honed people skills. I received a great deal of insight from listening to Pablo's contributions during this conversation, and I began to look forward to the month that I would be working in his church.

When that month arrived, I discovered that Pablo had volunteered to videotape all my lectures, which meant that he would be listening to all of them. All the classes were well attended, and Pablo didn't miss any of them.

When Pablo learned that I walked every day, he invited me to walk with him. Four or five days each week we walked together for an hour. That time we spent together gave me ample opportunity to get to know him. I learned early on that he had been highly successful in the business world. With an MBA from Northwestern University, one of the most prestigious business schools in America, he became a consultant for a national firm. Eventually he went on to develop his own business. In all his sharing with me, he was open, transparent, and real. Our friendship deepened by the day.

Rather early in our talks, he told me about the company that he had developed. He built into it covert Christian principles — honesty, fairness, an open-door policy that extended to all employees, and a spirit of hospitality. The company succeeded beyond his wildest projections. The growth of the value of the company stock, coupled with other investments, offered him the option to retire early. In less than six decades he had achieved a level of financial independence that gave him the freedom to move in any direction he chose. How could a man like Pablo discover his call, the will of God for his life?

Several years later I heard Pablo give a presentation, during which he mentioned that the month we shared together in his church had changed his life. His general faith had become more clearly focused; he had encountered the presence of God in a personal way. As a consequence of this clearer relationship with God, a variety of opportunities for his life had coalesced into a hunger for deeper meaning. Becoming the person God created him to be and doing what God intended him to do shaped his perspective and motivated his searching.

His search took numerous forms. First, he enrolled in a seminary within driving distance of his home. He began a program of study in leadership development, but after being engaged in that program for a year, he lost interest in its goals. They seemed to overlap with what he had already studied in business school. After taking a few courses in theology, he became fascinated with the subject and switched from the lay degree to the basic Master of Theology degree. This shift gave him ample opportunity to study subjects at the core of the Christian faith.

In addition to enrolling in a seminary, Pablo got connected with a new group in his church called "Companions." This group met once a month in small "subgroups" of four or five individuals who shared with each other whatever insight God gave them; their goal was discernment. Each participant reflected on what God had been doing in his or her life, shared that with others in the group, and sought their discerning responses and their prayers. This ministry of Pablo's church provided rich soil in which his desire to know God's will for him grew.

Another unusual opportunity presented itself to Pablo. His church gave handsomely to a ministry in India. The missions committee wanted a film made of that ministry that would show how their gifts were being used. When Pablo was given the opportunity to videotape the ministry in India, he accepted. Traveling to that Third World country, rubbing shoulders with the poor and seeing firsthand the difference that a little money could make — this experience had a powerful influence on him. His heart was being prepared for something — but what? He wasn't sure.

Pablo returned from this trip overseas close to the time that he was completing an agreement to sell his interest in the company that he had founded. These negotiations would put an enormous amount of money in his hands very quickly. What did this mean? How could he be faithful to God with this newfound wealth? After much questioning and searching, he decided to create a charitable foundation and fund it with some of his new wealth. Making this decision pressed Pablo to identify his interest in giving and to reaffirm God's claim upon his financial resources.

Four years after my first visit to Pablo's church, I had occasion to go to the West Coast for a few days, and I arranged to talk with him again. As we had done years before, we took a walk together. Our conversation centered on God's call and on discerning God's will. In my entire ministry I don't think I've ever known anyone who was more serious, more open, or more filled with yearning for God to show him what to do. Yet he was content to wait until the Voice spoke to him.

Let me ask you, my reader, what you would have said if Pablo had asked you, "What can I do to discover the call of God?" You might have consoled him in his waiting by reassuring him that God would be abundantly able to reveal the call to him when the time was right. Or you could have said, "Look, Pablo, you are doing the will of God — you've attended seminary, participated in a growth group, done missionary work, and undertaken charitable giving. Isn't this a call?" This may be true — but if this is God's intention, why is Pablo still driven to seek God's call? Where would you suggest he begin his search? What further preparation for a call could he make?

Recently Pablo's minister asked him about his quest. He explained to her where he was in the process. When she inquired what he was doing besides waiting, Pablo said, "I'm reviewing my life. I'm scanning my memory for evidence of God's intervention in my life, which may give me a clue about what God has for me to do." The minister pressed Pablo a bit further on the notion of a life review. In response Pablo said, "If the future is an extension of the past in a new form, then we ought to scan the contents of our memory. In the scan we should notice what we do well, what we like to do, and what others have told us we do well. These data would likely point to the kinds of things God might have in mind for us."

Pablo knows, as you and I know, that simply gathering data from our past doesn't equal a call from God. But he firmly believes, as I do, that recollecting in the way Saul did draws us closer to the place of hearing God's call.

Examining Some of the Ways God Calls Us

Perhaps you are like Pablo in some ways. Enough things have happened in your life to awaken you more deeply to God. And perhaps things have happened that cause you to think that God has something for you to do. Permit me to walk with you as we explore some of the ways that God speaks, ways that God calls out to us. As we move through the labyrinth of your memory, I'll suggest places to pause and listen for the Voice. Of course I can't create the Voice or force it to speak to you, and neither can you. Speaking and calling is the business of God. But I do think it's possible to lead a person to places where others have heard the Voice. I'll name some of the obvious places to pause as you scan your memory and share with you the manner of Godspeech in that particular place.

You may find yourself wondering what the past has to do with the future. Perhaps it has the same relationship that the soil has to roots, and roots to fruit. The past is most often preparation for shaping your passion for a certain kind of work, your skills, your experience, and your connections. Sometimes pain that you've suffered provides the ground for your passion and yearning. God's gifts also offer clues to your call. The memory scan will help you identify your gifts.

Since no one has yet invented an electronic device that will selectively record our memories, I believe it is important for you to record a current version of your life experiences, both those long past and those more recent. You may begin with a pen and notebook or a computer — whichever seems most natural for you. Adopt a receptive mode of listening when you're answering a question or when you're guided to reflect on certain experiences. Let the words come to you. Write what enters your consciousness without editing it or judging it. Take your time. Don't rush through these exercises.

In preparing to scan your memory, get yourself clearly situated in your life today and think about its different aspects. What's going on in your external world? What national events affect your life? What's happening in your work life? In your relationships with people outside your family? In your family? As you review these important aspects of your external world, listen deeply for the answers, then record what comes to you.

What's going on in your internal world? What's your attitude toward yourself? What are the visions you dream about? What conflicts are you experiencing? Does life seem good to you? Or do you have feelings of guilt and failure?

When you've finished writing responses to these questions, close your eyes and seek your personal center. Enter that quiet place and wait before God. As Thomas Merton advised, "Waste time with God."

Getting in touch with your present creates a self-conscious place in which you can listen for God. Once you're clearly situated in this place, you can begin to examine the past context of your life, to listen for God through your lived experiences. The exercises that follow are designed to help you do that. There are three ways to engage these exercises. You may read them simply for information. You may pause at each one and reflect on the matters explored. Or you may take each of the suggestions one at a time and record your reflections and answers to questions asked. The last approach will yield the greatest good for you.

1. God often speaks through an idea that emerges in our consciousness. We don't know exactly how such ideas come to us. Perhaps God has a thousand ways to place these thoughts in our minds.

Ideas are born from stimuli from both our internal and our external worlds of experience. In our external world, ideas come from reading, listening to the radio, watching television, having a conversation with a friend — and a thousand other stimuli. God uses these media in our external world to get our attention, to open us up for his Word to come to us. I believe that God speaks through the things that happen to us just as surely as he speaks through Scripture. For this reason I believe we ought to pay close attention to our lives.

But God also speaks in our inner world through the media of the deeper mind. Carl Jung speaks of levels of the mind: personal consciousness, the personal unconscious, and the collective unconscious. I believe that God often stimulates thoughts in our personal unconscious that flash upward into consciousness. Through this indirect approach, God can communicate with us in a way that doesn't destroy our personal freedom or humanness. God comes to us gently from the inside.

When Pablo's church asked him to go to India in order to film the work of the mission, was God in the invitation? Did God use the external medium of a missions committee to communicate an invitation to Pablo? When Pablo saw the poverty and suffering of the people and the good that the mission was doing, did this speak to him? When he sat quietly on the plane on the way home, where did his compassionate thoughts come from?

When you've written your answers to these questions, pause. Let your mind be free to receive insights and impressions from the review. Where do you think God might be involved in your present life? As you sit quietly before God at the center, what thoughts come to your mind?

2. In your external world, God often speaks to you through another person's affirmation of a gift that you've been given. God has given gifts to all the members of his family. Some of these gifts seem to be tied to creation. The genes were such that some of us came into the world with the capacity to play and write music, or a special capacity to show compassion and love.

We may also have been given a spiritual gift at the time of our baptism or our conversion. Spiritual gifts include the gift of faith, the gift of prophecy, the gift of healing, and the gift of administration. These gifts, freely given to us by God, inform, empower, and direct our ministry. Our gifts are often hidden from us until another sees and affirms them. Affirmation awakens us to our own giftedness.

Perhaps Pablo's gifts were redirected when a friend suggested to him that he might like to create a charitable foundation to assist others in their ministry. Maybe an outsider could see Pablo's gifts in ways that he couldn't. Yet when he created the foundation, he discovered that the gifts he had used successfully in business were also instruments of ministry.

I recognized his gifts of organization and administration on my very first visit to his church. The success of the time I spent in that congregation resulted from his thorough preparation.

What are the things that other people affirm in you? What do you do well? Record your answers and ask yourself if these affirmations point toward your gifts. Remember that God's call is to use the gifts he has given us.

3. God often speaks directly though a text in Scripture, and God always speaks in accordance with the teachings of Scripture. Scripture not only mediates our call but also is normative for God's call.

John Calvin emphasized the "inner testimony" of Scripture. He looked upon the words of Scripture as dead and meaningless until the Spirit of God moved upon them and made them alive to the reader's consciousness. This inner testimony personalized the text for the individual and enabled him or her to hear the Voice of God through the text of Scripture.

The text comes both from our reading and from our hearing. The presence of God comes through this text in the same way that light filters through a window or electricity flows through a copper wire. It is important that we don't confuse the energy with the conductor. God is not the window; God is the light. Neither is God the copper wire. God is the electricity, the energy and the power. Similarly, God is not the Bible. The Spirit comes though the Bible to call and direct us.

I once met an Englishman who came to this country because of his work. In Great Britain he had been an occasional churchgoer, but for some reason he had never experienced the reality of what church should be. As he began to settle into his job here in the States, he also found a church to attend. That's when Scripture came alive for him. He told me that each Sunday, as the minister spoke the message of the text, it came straight to him, entered his consciousness, and began its transforming work. "Some Sundays," he said, "I felt embarrassed to be walking out of church with tears rolling down my cheeks." God's call to him was mysteriously hidden in the text that was being proclaimed.

The text has this effect when the Spirit illuminates it. Like a piece of coal that is red-hot, the text gives off light and heat. The light and the heat eventually consume the coal. The Spirit of God comes through the text but, unlike the coal, the text is not consumed. After it gives off light and heat in one reading or hearing, it still remains to speak to us again and again.

As part of scanning your memory, think back over your experience with reading Scripture or hearing it read and proclaimed. Do you recall a time that the message of the text seemed addressed specifically to you? Have there been times when you felt drawn to God or drawn to a ministry through the reading of the text?

As a part of this exercise, read about the call of Samuel three times. Read slowly and reflectively. Listen to what this text says to you.

> Now the boy Samuel was ministering to the LORD under Eli. The word of the LORD was rare in those days; visions were not widespread. At that time Eli, whose eyesight had begun to grow dim so that he could not see, was lying down in his room; the lamp of God had not yet gone out, and Samuel was lying down in the temple of the LORD, where the ark of God was.

Then the LORD called, "Samuel! Samuel!" and he said, "Here I am!" and ran to Eli, and said, "Here I am, for you called me." But he said, "I did not call; lie down again." So he went and lay down. The LORD called again, "Samuel!" Samuel got up and went to Eli, and said, "Here I am, for you called me." But he said, "I did not call, my son; lie down again."

Now Samuel did not yet know the LORD, and the word of the LORD had not yet been revealed to him. The LORD called Samuel again, a third time. And he got up and went to Eli, and said, "Here I am, for you called me." Then Eli perceived that the LORD was calling the boy.

Therefore Eli said to Samuel, "Go, lie down; and if he calls you, you shall say, 'Speak, LORD, for your servant is listening.'" So Samuel went and lay down in his place. Now the LORD came and stood there, calling as before, "Samuel! Samuel!" And Samuel said, "Speak, for your servant is listening." (1 Samuel 3:1-10)

4. God often calls when we come face-to-face with human pain. Suffering has long been the medium of God's call. What is there about human suffering that opens us to God? Does pain cause us to contemplate our own mortality? Do we see our own children in the tortured, lifeless body of a child killed in Kosovo? Do we recall our own pain when we read of children being abused or abandoned by their parents? Does an encounter with suffering children reveal our helplessness in the face of our own pain and that of others? These feelings of compassion and pain are so sharp and disturbing that we must turn the newspaper page, switch the TV to another channel, or stop listening to the sermon. When we finally get the courage to really look and listen, the pain that we see in others becomes the medium of God's call to us.

When I visited Guatemala and Nicaragua, I remember looking into the faces of scores of widows. Their husbands had been rounded up like cattle and driven from their villages; the army had murdered them and dumped their bodies into a common grave. These widows had known a kind of pain that I would never know, yet they were joyful and radiant in the midst of their pain. Somehow their suffering cried out to me, and I wonder if the voice of God was speaking to me through their agony. How can anyone look in the faces of these widows and not feel an urge to help them? Isn't God speaking to us through the pain that we behold before us? And does the pain that we've suffered in our past form the ground of a call for us today?

And what about the pain that isn't so easily detected or is perhaps less dramatic? It's easy to see the obviously abused and deprived and become blind to the couple next door who make a comfortable income, travel as they wish, and decorate their home lavishly in the most contemporary fashion. But hidden behind this beautiful front is a marriage in shambles. The couple's bed holds two estranged people, conversation is at an impasse, and loneliness reigns. When we can see their emptiness and hurt, doesn't God speak to us through their need?

Think back over the past month and try to recall all the situations of human pain that you've encountered. Picture each situation in your mind. Begin to write about your feelings. "When I saw or met or heard about . . . I felt. . . ." If you can't recall meeting a beggar on the street or hearing a plea for help in a friend's voice or reading about child abuse or some other form of human hurt, perhaps you should pray to God to make you more aware of your world.

5. God speaks to us not only through the pain of others but also through our own pain. As you continue to scan your memory, identify the deepest trauma of your life. Sometimes the Voice is immediate at the very moment or shortly after a moment of trauma. A car accident, for example, brings into sharp focus the meaning and direction of a person's life. Perhaps facing the possibility of one's own death prods one into receptivity to God's call. These moments do become media for a call. But this memory scan rests on a different assumption.

I believe that our own pain often becomes the training ground that shapes the call God extends to us. It is as though the pain is the school that we attend for the ministry we are to have. A woman's husband dies of Alzheimer's disease, and after having spent strenuous years caring for him, she feels a call to work with Alzheimer groups in the community. A man experiences a painful divorce, and his call becomes to work with divorce-recovery groups. A woman who experienced child abuse may feel called to work with abused children to help them understand their suffering. One man with whom I have spoken walked with his wife through cancer and death, and out of that experience God called him to minister to people with cancer and to family members who were dealing with the loss that death would bring. Personal pain becomes the training ground for ministry.

I wonder if Jesus was marginalized because of his birth, and if this was the ground for his including the marginalized in his ministry? I wonder if Barnabas experienced the depths of despair, and if this is how he learned the art of encouragement and was thus renamed the "son of consolation"? I wonder if Paul's denial of Jesus and his persecution of the church became the ground out of which he was called to be the "apostle to the Gentiles"?

Of course, personal pain doesn't indicate a call in every instance, either in Paul's case or in ours. Simply because you've suffered in a particular way doesn't mean that you should automatically engage in a helping ministry to assist others like yourself. Nevertheless, in an uncommon number of instances those who have experienced a certain kind of pain have been called to assist others who suffer the same fate. For this reason I do encourage you to review the traumatic experiences of your life and listen for God around the edges of these painful memories.

What painful memories do you have that refuse to go away? Contemplate the various occurrences that brought on this pain. As you think about this woundedness in your soul, does it spark feelings in you still? Is there something you'd like to do for those who suffer the same fate?

Walking gently and quietly on these grounds of personal pain can open you to a call. It seems increasingly clear to me that God calls us to minister to others out of our own brokenness. As you reflect on your traumatic experience, do you feel drawn to those who have suffered your fate?

6. Stirrings of the soul are often God's whispered beckonings. Think back over your lifetime of experiences. Can you identify times when you felt really close to God? During those times, did you feel that God had something for you to do? These yearnings or stirrings in the

soul, whether past or present, echo a movement in your inner depths. A yearning or stirring may act like a thermometer, signaling that the soul is unwell. Or the stirring may be like an appetite, a hunger that announces itself when nourishment has been delayed or withheld.

What do you make of Pablo's interest in missions, in small non-profit organizations, and in serving on the boards of missionary organizations? Does the yearning he feels to help those in need relate in any way to God's call? And where is God in Pablo's yearning for a ministry? Is there indeed something greater for Pablo to do other than what he is presently doing?

Recall moments in your life when you felt these stirrings of the soul — an awakening of a life dream, a desire to help those in need, or a desire to make a difference. Write freely about those moments; don't edit your thoughts as they come. When you've finished, read over your account and try to see what God is saying to you.

7. The prelude to a call from God often takes the form of restlessness. Our dis-ease with our situation is often related to our work. We complain that it doesn't fulfill us as it once did. The routine is boring; the days are long. Frustration sets in, and no matter what we do, satisfaction escapes us. We press on the accelerator of life to speed up in order to keep from noticing our inner confusion. Sometimes we go from one job to another, from one vacation to another, and even from one affair to another. But these actions all fail to still the soul.

Many people assume that if someone's life has become routine and boring, he or she has drifted outside the realm of God's call. Not so! I believe that a spiritual restlessness signals the encroachment of the Spirit on a person's life. It is God's way of beginning to unhitch us from old securities and worn-out identities. As these old connections break down and our tight-fitting masks peel off, we often slip into the pit of meaninglessness.

The pit of meaninglessness may actually be the best place for us to hear God speak. It puts us in a position of dependence; it humbles us and opens us to new possibilities. Even change and newness are less threatening than emptiness. And this experience of the void has an amazing power to grab our attention. Most of us find it easier to listen when we're forced to see the emptiness of our ways. God speaks meaning into the void, and our life changes.

I saw a dramatic example of this in Cao — a Chinese man who had been in the United States for only six months. He had been educated in China but had always felt the Communist regime was oppressive; he was never committed to the Communist vision. Nevertheless, he worked his way up through the system. His last job in the system, as manager of a plant in North China, led him to a place where he felt his work was meaningless. At his lowest point, he had an opportunity to work for a U.S. company that subsequently transferred him to the United States. The first thing he did in the States was to become a Christian and join a church. As a new Christian, he wanted to talk about his desire to serve God and to answer God's call, even though he faced numerous obstacles. Do you see how God drew Cao into a vocation out of his feelings of meaninglessness in his work?

And what about Pablo? He has succeeded financially, he has sought to learn about his faith, and he has begun a significant ministry. Still, he knows that his call has not been made clear yet. So he is restless.

When you reviewed what you wrote about where you are in your life, did you discover any restlessness? Give special attention to this feeling. Begin your writing here with this question: "O God, why do I feel restless about . . . ?"

8. At times God calls in such a gentle way that the engagement feels quite natural and undramatic. When God calls in this way, any profound sense of call often goes unnoticed. Take what you're presently doing; for example, trace the things that inform your present activity. Did you plan and develop all of these relationships and experiences? Did you know at the time they occurred that you were being prepared for the task that you're now doing? Does it sometimes seem that God's hand has been active in your development? Do you have a sense of God in your daily vocation?

I ask this last question because I believe that many of us, if not most of us, have simply responded to the next opportunity or taken the next step in life without much reflection and without any drama. In these instances we so easily lose the sense of God's call and God's action in our lives. This loss seems tragic for us and for God. It is tragic for us because we spend our days without a sense of connectedness to the Ultimate Reference. And it is tragic for God because he misses our praise and thanks for the direction and care he gives us.

Perhaps you could recover the sense of God's gentle intervention if you took the time to look more closely at your present vocation. Begin, for example, by sorting out the various tasks you perform on any given day in your work. Describe the attitude with which you perform them. Think about why you are where you are, doing these tasks. With these specifics in mind, look back over your life and envision the faces of those people who helped you along the way. Think of the events and experiences that brought you to this place. Are all these accidents of existence, or is there some kind of purpose at work in the world that gathers your life into it?

I'm sure that Pablo will one day look back and see innumerable ways in which God's hand has guided his life. Each of these gentle intrusions is shaping him for the ministry that lies before him. His early training was in the Catholic Church, instruction that gave him grounding in the faith, whether or not he was responsive to it. A bad first marriage made its own contribution. Meeting and marrying his present wife, who shares his passion for God and for ministry to broken people, has given him added strength to pursue his call. In addition to these influences, there have been several ministers who have played prominent roles in his life. And a close friend or two has spoken to him at the proper time. Following the hunger of his heart led him to seminary and to several opportunities for growth in his church. When the call he awaits comes with clarity and rearranges his life, he will see God's hand in all these influences.

As you scan your vocational memory, can you get a sense that you are where you are and doing what you're doing because God has been whispering a call to you for a very long time?

9. Sometimes a call originates in an experience as simple as an invitation by another to share in an existing ministry. Like the unconscious convergence of events that have gotten us to a particular place in our vocation, the simple invitation of another person to engage in a ministry

may be the voice of God's call. Take Bob, for example, who had been active in his church for years. He sang in the choir, taught voice lessons, and even directed the choir from time to time. About the time he was going to retire, his friend Tom asked him to help build a Habitat for Humanity house. Without hesitation, Bob agreed. He's become the most enthusiastic construction foreman you would want to meet.

I'm not certain that Bob would use the language of God's call to describe his present ministry of leading the Habitat program in his church. But he is the director, and he leads with a passion. Even when the language of call isn't used, the fact of call still remains.

The breadth of God's call sometimes astounds me. I have a good friend who's a golfing buddy of mine. He reads my books before I send them to the publisher. We have stimulating conversations — sometimes provocative because he frequently attempts to shock me.

Rick's religious background includes some bad memories of childhood years spent in mainline churches. As an adult he's been turned off by the hypocrisy of the institutional church, and he's done a fair amount of "church shopping" on the fringes of Christianity. He isn't a person who speaks intimately about his religious experiences.

Recently he's become interested in a ministry to the homeless. First he volunteered; then he assisted the director; after a few months, he was asked to serve on the board. At that point he invited me to talk with him and the director about fund-raising for the ministry, a way that I could help him make a contribution (no pun intended) to that important ministry.

After that meeting, he and I were playing golf one day. "How did you become interested in this ministry to homeless people?" I asked him.

"A friend of mine who used to live in our neighborhood told me that the ministry was short on volunteers, and he asked if I could help out. I said that I could."

"And when you came face-to-face with the needs that were being met," I interpreted, "you felt that you couldn't leave the ministry in the lurch."

He nodded.

45

"What would you say," I asked, "if I told you that God has called you to this ministry?"

To my surprise, he answered, "I would agree." This man who didn't make intimate comments on his religious life was recognizing a call!

Perhaps as you walk the labyrinth of your memory, you too will discover that someone asked you to help out in a particular situation, and you complied. Maybe you've been called without recognizing it, or maybe you know that God is involved in what you're doing but have never labeled it a "call."

To awaken your call or to rename your ministry, review the times that people have invited you to share in a ministry. Did God's call come to you through someone who cared both for you and for a task that needed to be done?

There is no way to chronicle all the ways in which God calls us. But the listing here should provide a helpful sampling of the variety of God's ways with us. I hope that I've provided you with helpful ideas for productively scanning your memory. I hope they'll give you a way to listen to what's currently going on in your life as well as a way to "listen back" through your life to get hints of God's encroachment on it.

Exercises in Discernment

1. Return to your lifeline. Search your life for each of the various media of God's call. Add additional hash marks for the times when the following occurred in your life:
   - The idea of a call came into your mind.
   - A person affirmed a gift God had given you.
   - A text from Scripture spoke to you about God's call.
   - You saw the pain of others and wondered what you could do to help.
   - Your own experience of pain drew you to others suffering the same kind of pain.
   - You felt very close to God.

46

- You felt restless in your work.
- You noticed that your life was being shaped by a series of "gentle calls" from God.
- Someone invited you to join an existing ministry.

After searching your life for these God moments, sit quietly before God. Listen to the thoughts that come into your mind, then record them.

2. Prayerfully re-read the story of Samuel's call cited in this chapter.

3. Another brief way to scan your memory is by creating a kind of "gifts grid" and then reflecting on your discoveries. On a sheet of paper, create your own grid with three columns with three headings: (1) What I do well, (2) What I enjoy doing, and (3) What others say that I do well.

   When you've finished creating this grid and filling it in, read over what you've written slowly and reflectively. Close your eyes prayerfully and be present to the ideas that come to you. After a few moments, record what comes to you.

4. When you've completed these exercises, reflect on your discoveries and write a short paragraph describing what you think God may be calling you to do. Writing it down doesn't constitute a commitment, but it does give you clarity.

CHAPTER FOUR

The Fingerprints of God

"How do I know that my experience is of God?" This is the major question asked by many of us who are seeking to discern God's call. None of us wants to look foolish or be led astray by our own hidden, deceptive desires. We want to know that we are responding to a genuine call from God, not simply responding to a compulsion arising from some unconscious need or illusion.

While our skepticism in this post-Enlightenment era may be greater than that of the first-century disciples, it is not a new phenomenon. The biblical writers give us the story of Thomas and his doubts. He wasn't with the disciples when Jesus appeared to them after his resurrection. When he heard that Jesus was alive, Thomas said, "Unless I see the mark of the nails in his hands, and put my finger in the mark of the nails and my hand in his side, I will not believe!" Our scientific culture has taught us to think like that, to seek verifiable data through sensory impressions. Because this mode of verification has enabled great advancements in science and medicine, we naturally fall back on it as our approach to certitude in discerning God's call. Like Thomas, we too cry out, "Show us the signs of the nails and the spear, that we may believe!"

When Jesus showed the signs to Thomas, he cried out, "My Lord and my God!" Our lives are certainly marked by divine fingerprints, but Jesus seldom shows us such vivid signs today. But simply because he

48

doesn't appear to us in this dramatic, miraculous manner doesn't imply that he is absent. He is very much present, but his presence demands a different kind of verification, perhaps one of faith and trust in place of seeing and feeling. In the larger scheme of things, there are other ways of verification that are just as trustworthy as Thomas's experience, and perhaps more appropriate. To explain this assertion, I'll take us through three ways of knowing. Knowing that God is speaking to us is, after all, what discernment of call is all about.

Ways of Knowing

The Way of the Enlightenment

Thomas's intense yearning for certitude was similar to the intense desire for certainty that propelled the Age of Reason in the seventeenth and eighteenth centuries. Centuries of tradition as well as the church's effort to control knowledge and thought had kept Reason in chains for nearly a thousand years. When Reason cast off these chains, she went in search of verifiable knowledge. How did these truth seekers approach the task of knowing?

The Enlightenment approach to knowledge was based on sensory experience. According to Enlightenment theory, all reality could be verified and demonstrated. This point of view fueled the scientific approach, which says that truth begins with sensory experience that can be analyzed, categorized, and repeated. Reason takes the data of sensory experience, forms hypotheses that can be proved by experiments, and creates a body of dependable knowledge. Any so-called knowledge that doesn't rest on this foundation is suspect and is classified as mere opinion.

If the scientific approach bequeathed to us by the Age of Reason constitutes the only approach to reality, then by definition God is ruled out. So this approach to knowledge simply doesn't work with respect to God because God isn't a sensory object open to our observation and experimentation. Although God is reasonable, reason alone cannot capture God. All the efforts of reason to grasp, define, and contain God merely serve to turn ideas about God into idols. Human reason can attain nothing more than concepts because the true knowledge of God demands experience that surpasses the limits of reason.

Furthermore, if the quest for God and for God's will could be reduced to a scientific formula, there would be no need for faith. Whether or not they acknowledge it, scientific researchers have a kind of faith — faith in the trustworthiness of nature — but this faith has difficulty opening itself to the Ultimate Reality behind the sensory data. So this rational, objective, controlled approach to certitude can provide persuasive data, but the kind of certitude for which the heart hungers demands commitment and trust.

Science and religious faith deal with different aspects of reality. Science asks "how," and religion asks "why." These two approaches to truth need not be placed in conflict, but each should address the kinds of questions that arise from these different realms of knowing. When either denies the other legitimacy in its particular field, it does so from its own premises. Confusion and needless conflict follow.

The Way of Relationship

Having ruled out the scientific approach as a model for seeking knowledge about God's will for us, let's consider the relational model as a mode of knowing God and God's will for us. How did I get to know my mother, for example? Did I gather sensory data, form hypotheses, and test them until I had a firm body of knowledge? Or was my knowledge of her derived from a relationship that began and grew through shared experiences until I knew her well enough to predict what she would say and do in almost any situation?

I came to know Cammie Johnson, my mother, through her acts of love and sacrifice for me. I grew by responding to her words of encouragement as well as her challenges to me. Trusting her initiatives in my life laid a foundation for developing my knowledge of her. As my trust grew, I increasingly followed her direction and her wishes. My certitude was based not on scientific research but on the consistency of a loving, caring relationship.

The relational approach to knowledge contrasts significantly with the Enlightenment approach. Unlike the cold, objective rationality of Enlightenment knowledge, relational knowledge manifests itself as warm, subjective, and personal. So the Enlightenment way of knowing has aided us in understanding the physical universe, but it is deficient in helping us to understand and relate to God, to God's intention for the world and God's call to us. If we're dealing with a personal God who calls us personally to engage in the Divine Purpose for the world, we need a relational model of knowing to complement a purely rational way of knowing. The rational model gives us "the how"; the relational model gives us "the why." The strength of the relational model stems from its focus on the personal aspects of knowing untouched by logic.

The Way of Revelation

Revelation as a mode of knowing offers yet another way of certitude for the Christian believer. In the rational model of knowing, the human mind is active, seeking data, observing detail, formulating and testing hypotheses; in the revelational model of knowing, human reason is aware, focused, and receptive. Revelation presents data to the mind, often spontaneously, with a conviction that approaches certitude. Suddenly there is insight, knowledge that has been given rather than knowledge that has been discovered.

Paul Tillich speaks of revelation as an ecstatic experience. By "ecstatic" he means that the human spirit stands outside of itself and looks at itself as something strange or different. According to Tillich, the Holy Spirit invades the human spirit and drives it out of itself for a momentary union with the Ultimate — God. This momentary, intuitive experience yields knowledge of God that is compelling in its power. In my conversations with men and women who seem to be struggling with a call from God, I note that many of them have had some type of encounter with the Holy. For one person that experience came through a car accident; for another, through a shared personal witness; and for still others, through unexpected events when they were neither searching for nor expecting an encounter with God.

In our quest for the knowledge of God's call, the rational model may provide insight into the structure of reality, and it may enlarge our vision of the purposes of God, but it doesn't lead us down the path of discernment. While good for many types of research, the rational model oversteps its boundaries if it seeks to create a relationship with God or disclose God's will. Discernment requires a posture of receptivity rather than analysis; it seeks integration, not separation; it rests on subjective passion rather than external, objective data. The rational approach seeks to operate with detachment, and discernment calls for commitment to God's direction.

The relational model of knowledge is congruent with the religious search for certitude in a call and also with the religious search for meaning. Understanding that the Ultimate Reality is personal and deals with us as persons grounds our quest. We come to know God by listening to his call, responding to his wishes for us, and worshipping him. Nurturing our relationship with God both strengthens and clarifies our call.

As we journey in our call, God often reveals Godself to us in inexplicable ways. The mystery of God spills over and embraces us. Our insight rises to a new level. There is that moment when we know ourselves loved and claimed by God, and this moment of God's revelation fuels our vision and energizes us.

Why does the Holy One make it so difficult for us to clearly discern his call? Before we blame God for all the difficulty, perhaps we should ask if our resistance muddles the picture. Or does our lack of listening impede our progress? Perhaps our ignorance of what God has shown his people through the ages is another block to our certitude of faith.

With respect to our call, Enlightenment certitude doesn't exist. No device has been invented that can predict either the validity or the outcome of our call. Such knowledge would change the nature of Christian faith and obedience. Like a mother, God desires our loving trust, not our analytical certitude. Trust strengthens the relationship with God; analysis severs it and makes us independent agents rather than loving servants.

No doubt God could reveal our call in an unmistakable way. God has the power to do whatever he desires and wills. If God came to us face-to-face and expressed the divine intention for our lives, however, it would rob us of our freedom — for who can withstand God? But God doesn't choose to change us into robots. In revealing himself to us, he has taken special care to preserve our humanity and to leave the door open for trust.

I suggest that we have the certitude of both loving God and being loved by God, and this relational certitude guarantees that God always wills the best for us. As we then live in this relational certitude, how do we recognize the ways of God and the mode of his personal communication to us? If this discussion of ways of knowing has seemed too abstract to you, perhaps a story can make the idea more concrete.

Daniel: A Man Whom God Touched

Earlier I spoke briefly about Daniel's call to a lay ministry, but a more complete exploration of his experience will illustrate the fingerprints of God marking his life. I met Daniel on one of my visits to his church, where I was working for a month. During our planning sessions, I noted that he had a strong interest in the church and a desire to be of service in whatever way he could. His enthusiasm made me want to talk with him further, to find out what lay behind his contagious witness. So I approached him and arranged to meet with him.

When Daniel and I got together to talk, he told me that he had been a nominal church member until about two years ago. He had been baptized and raised in the church, and had taken part in many of the church's activities. Others would have looked upon him as a regular member.

In his college days and thereafter, he had taught school, coached football, and worked in the family business. At the time we spoke, he was working in the family-owned company. He was married and had a couple of children.

After describing his background, he came to the life-changing incident that set him on an intentional journey. A friend asked his company to purchase a table at a Fellowship of Christian Athletes dinner. The company agreed to pick up the tab, and Daniel decided to attend the dinner because Bobby Bowden, coach of the Florida State Seminoles, was the guest speaker. Daniel had always admired Bowden and figured the talk would be motivational.

After dinner one of the local coaches gave a personal testimony to his faith, and Bowden spoke afterward. He was well received. But strangely, God didn't use the talk of the featured speaker to reach Daniel; he used the testimony of the local coach instead. This coach told the group about a dream he had had. In the dream he had died and gone to heaven, but when he looked outside the heavenly gates, there sat one of his daughters. She was crying and said, "Daddy, you taught me how to tie my shoes, you helped me learn to ride a bicycle, and you supported me when I was playing soccer. But Daddy, you never taught me about Jesus." The coach then spoke about his feeling of responsibility to raise his children in the faith.

There was something in what the coach said and the way he said it that took hold of Daniel. "I was convicted," he told me. God used the simple testimony of a man respected in the community to penetrate the religious and cultural armor that for years had effectively protected Daniel from having a vital faith in Christ. He went home miserable.

For three successive nights after that dinner, Daniel couldn't sleep. Rather than toss and turn, he got up and read the Bible. He discovered a metaphor in Paul's letter to the Corinthian church that spoke to him. Paul affirmed that Jesus Christ was the foundation of life and that there were various materials one uses to build on that foundation — gold, silver, and precious stones, or wood, hay, and straw (1 Cor. 3:11-15). At the end of time, what has been built will be tested by fire, and only those whose works survive the fire will be rewarded.

Daniel's understanding of the Bible was limited, but this message made clear to him that the way he spent his life was crucial. The Bible had challenged his values and his priorities; it also introduced him to a world of enchantment, and he couldn't get enough of it. Every evening after his family went to bed, he stayed up and read the Bible until one or two in the morning. His life became saturated with Scripture.

After Daniel had been attentive to God for about six months, a strange thing happened to him. The Voice said, "Stop by the church and encourage your minister." The thought was strong and persistent, but Daniel felt that following his intuition would be risky. He didn't want his pastor or his friends to see him as a fanatic. Yet because of the inward insistence of the Voice, he stopped by the church.

He asked the minister how things were going. To his surprise, the minister said that he had been a bit discouraged. The previous week, when he had led the closing worship service for a renewal weekend, the church had been packed. Where had everyone been this Sunday? Daniel listened sympathetically and suggested that maybe he and the minister could trust God with the results.

This experience made Daniel recognize that Someone was indeed "messing with his life" and that he should continue paying attention to the things that were happening around him. As Daniel's life was being renewed, he began to read about leadership and the renewal of Christ's church. He talked to the local bookstore manager about a book that he had found particularly helpful. As it turned out, the author of that book lived quite close to Daniel's home. Imagine his surprise when an assistant to the author called and invited Daniel to play golf with him and the author. (The bookstore manager had told the assistant about Daniel's enthusiasm for the book.) Again this newly awakened Christian felt that he was living in the spiritual world of the Bible, where God acted in human situations.

During the next few months, Daniel's faith grew, and his expectations rose. As he moved more deeply into the world of the Spirit, his interest in others deepened. He first thought about friends who were unaware of the spiritual dimension of life. Ray, a friend he had known all his life, kept coming to his mind, and he began praying for him. Like the directive to encourage his minister, the thought of speaking with Ray came to him repeatedly. But before he got around to calling Ray, Ray called him. As it happened, Ray was in town and wanted to have lunch. Over lunch, with some hesitancy, Daniel told Ray that he hoped Ray wouldn't think him a fanatic, but he he wanted to talk about how his life had changed.

When Daniel finished telling his story, Ray said, "I'm glad you told me about this. I've been searching for answers in my life too. In fact, last Sunday I went to church to worship for the first time in twenty years. Until then I'd only gone for weddings and funerals." It seemed clear that God was working in Ray at the same time Daniel was praying for him. Daniel's conviction that God was working in him and through him kept deepening.

This growing ability to speak with others about his faith led Daniel to recognize that he was being called to work with ordinary people. Nothing gave him greater joy than seeing another person enter into a new relationship with God. In this regard, he told me about the changed life of one of the salesmen who worked for his company. He spoke in some detail of a young man he had met recently who had had a near-death experience. He had had a bad accident with the truck he was driving, and it caught fire. He found himself trapped under the flaming wreckage — and he noticed gasoline dripping to the ground. Miraculously, he was spared, and he felt instinctively that God had delivered him, even though he knew nothing about God or about the Bible. Daniel had formed a small Bible-study group to nurture him in the faith.

At the time that I spoke with Daniel, he was reviewing his gifts, and he discovered that two of his primary gifts were imagination and creativity. He designed Italian rugs for the family company, and he explained to me how he could visualize those rugs before anyone ever drew patterns of them. He thought that he could use this same gift to envision the future and the ministry that he was to have. Shortly after this awareness came to him, Daniel began to feel an urge to develop a training institute for laypeople. He shared this vision with trusted friends, and they affirmed it. Now he's waiting to see God's hand — God's fingerprints — more clearly.

I don't think I've ever talked to a young man with greater humility. Daniel is certain that the call working in him doesn't arise from his own talents or abilities. He takes no credit for what is occurring. He believes that he's being acted upon and used by One greater than he. His wife recently asked him why God had chosen him. He had no answer; he was as dumbfounded by this turn of events as she was. But Daniel goes on listening for God and loving him every day, seeking to do the things to which God directs him.

Daniel's experience vividly illustrates God's work of calling lay-persons today. It demonstrates concretely some of God's ways with us. As I relate this story and others, I'm aware that all of us have different encounters with God. But a composite of call stories will surely paint a clearer picture of how God's call can occur.

The Signs of God's Activity

As Daniel related his story to me, it seemed that his life had the finger-prints of God all over it. The prints were clear in a dozen places. Al-though my story and yours may differ greatly from Daniel's, God's in-tervention in our lives has left its marks. As we review our lives and as we seek verification that our call is from God, how do we identify and evaluate these marks of the Divine Presence?

One of the best books that I've read on vocational discernment is entitled *Listening Hearts: Discerning Call in Community,* co-authored by Suzanne G. Farnham, Joseph P. Gill, R. Taylor McLean, and Susan M. Ward.[1] They identify clarity, persistence, peace, and the convergence of life events (among others) as signs of God's call, the fingerprints of God upon our lives. These are several of the traditional marks of God's activ-ity; I would add to this list progression, conviction, and ecstasy. To claim a call or to identify God at work in your life, you don't need all of these signs. But it's highly unlikely that your call will exclude all of them. As I reflect on each of these signs with you, use my comments as a mirror to see if any of these signs show up in your experience.

---

1. Suzanne G. Farnham et al., *Listening Hearts* (Harrisburg, Pa.: Morehouse Pub-lishing, 1991).

Clarity

When it's authentic, the call of God doesn't come to us in a fuzzy, unintelligible form. Sometimes it can come in startlingly clear form, like God's direction to Saul of Tarsus: "Get up and enter the city, and you will be told what you are to do" (Acts 9:6). Similarly, Daniel's initial call to seek God by reading Scripture was clear and compelling. But not all calls are this clear and specific.

Where are you in your discernment of call? If your call is unclear at first, wait to respond, but don't use vagueness as a reason to procrastinate.

Persistence

When God calls, the call comes continuously or at least repeatedly. It's never a flash in the pan that disappears in a short period of time. We need not fear that God will depart if we don't hear the call at first. After all, Jesus has told us, "Listen! I am standing at the door, knocking" (Rev. 3:21). In Daniel's case, God's Spirit spoke at first through a coach at a banquet, and then the Voice of the Spirit kept speaking inside him, drawing Daniel into Scripture. Most of us who have had dealings with God know that he doesn't give up easily. How persistent is God's call to you today?

Progression

A progressive call is one that meets us where we are in our lives. God speaks to us in our present context in order to guide us where he wishes us to be. The story of Peter in Luke 5:1-11 provides an excellent example of this unfolding call. Peter's brother had brought him to Jesus for early conversations. Then Jesus encountered him washing his nets after an unsuccessful night of fishing. After Jesus oversaw the miraculous catch of fish, he invited Peter to become a learner, a "fisher of men," and follow him. During the next three years Jesus provided Peter with an apprenticeship. The Gospels tell this story, each in its own way.

Nothing is more obvious in Daniel's story than the gradual unfolding of his call, with each step feeling a bit more demanding. Do you see the progressive unfolding of events in your life leading you from one experience of God's will to another?

Congruence of Call and Circumstance

I believe that when God has called us to a ministry, there will be congruence between our inner sense of call and our outward circumstances. When God calls, he opens doors. He brings the right people into our lives. A friend of mine has witnessed that when God calls us to a task, things fall into place — and that when they don't, it's time to pause. She explains, "My experience has taught me that when we have difficulty putting things into place, God may be giving us a 'wait' signal." What kind of signals are you getting?

Convergence of Events

This sign of God's presence can be seen only when we've been on our journey for a while. Convergence points to a "coming together" of influences or choices that seem to be more than mere coincidence. Take the case of Saul of Tarsus. Was it purely accidental that he was born in a Roman province and was thus a Roman citizen? Was it coincidence that he sat on top of a hill observing the stoning of Stephen? Was his diligent study with the greatest scholar of his day a happenstance? Or was there divine providence at work in his life from his earliest days?

Consider Daniel's experiences in the same way. Was it sheer luck that Daniel's company contributed to the banquet and that he decided to attend? Wasn't God's hand clear in the planning of the event, so that before the featured speaker gave his presentation, a local coach spoke just the right word for Daniel to hear? Others have also discerned God's hand in their lives most clearly as events have converged. In Daniel's case, isn't his friend Ray a part of converging events? Daniel had been thinking about getting in touch with Ray. And Ray, after attending church for the first time in twenty years, had been thinking about Daniel and came to town for a visit. Over lunch Daniel spoke to Ray about his faith, and Ray was moved. As you think about your life and your sense of call, do you see any such convergence of events in your life?

Conviction

This sign suggests an intuitive knowing that originates in an encounter with God. It has a close affinity with the revelational way of knowing that we discussed earlier. When you try to explain your convictional knowledge, logic and process fail because the knowledge didn't come to you that way. In convictional knowledge, you know simply because you know. Earlier I referred to the story of Peter and the miraculous catch of fish. Recall that when Jesus is in the boat with Peter and the others, he tells them to let down their nets in the deep water, even though they have caught nothing all night. They obey — and their nets come up bursting with fish. This is the moment when Peter is gripped by conviction. Suddenly the awareness comes over him that by following this man's instruction, he has caught abundant fish where there were no fish just hours before. He has more than a suspicion that Jesus is no ordinary man, and he falls at Jesus' knees and worships.

In Daniel's case, what logical reason could he give for visiting his minister? There wasn't a series of events that led to his dropping by the church for a visit. The notion to visit his minister and offer him encouragement was an idea that just came spontaneously into his mind. At first the idea seemed foolish to him, but the idea persisted, and Daniel relented. The result of the visit justified his taking the chance to do what he believed God was telling him to do. What about you? Is conviction at work in your life?

Peace

By "peace" I mean an inner calm about the decision you've made or are about to make. *Shalom* is the personal state out of which we should make our decisions, for it is the realm of God. Jesus promised, "Peace I leave with you; my peace I give to you. I do not give to you as the world gives. Do not let your hearts be troubled, and do not let them be afraid" (John 14:27). Saint Ignatius spoke of the experience of consolation. What he meant by consolation relates very closely to the Hebrew concept of *shalom* — the fullness of life and peace.

When Daniel told me his story, I pictured a superficial church member who became quite distraught as he listened to testimony from a high-school coach, and who then diligently sought peace with God. When I met Daniel, he was indeed a man who was at peace with himself and who was making peace with others. As you contemplate God's call in your life, are you at peace with your decisions?

Ecstasy

Paul Tillich's definition of ecstasy as "standing outside yourself and looking back at yourself as something strange," while helpful, may not be an entirely adequate definition. Others would define ecstasy as being blessed by God, experiencing the presence of the Holy Spirit, being filled with the Spirit, or being given a revelation or being in the Spirit. These phrases point to an experience of the holy that ultimately defies explanation. Nevertheless, this moment of ecstasy marks a time in your life that functions as a kind of dividing line, so that you recall life before and after it occurred. This experience of ecstasy doesn't accompany every call. But when it does occur, the call often seems deeper and more secure.

Certainly the experience of Saul on the road to Damascus has an ecstatic quality. His spirit is invaded by the presence of the risen Christ, who speaks directly to him. Later in his life, Saul — by then Paul — points to this experience as the foundation of his call and the inspiration for his work. (See Acts 26:12-18.)

Paul also writes to the Corinthian Christians about his experience of visions and revelations. At one point he describes an out-of-body experience in which he is caught up into the third heaven and hears unutterable things that no man can repeat. No doubt such ecstatic experiences deepened his faith and empowered his ministry. These encounters with the transcendent, involving a convictional way of knowing, authenticated his ministry.

Daniel's experience by no means matches Peter's or Paul's, but can you imagine what was transpiring in him during those nights that he read the Bible until one or two in the morning? On one occasion when Daniel and I were talking, he said, "I think the Lord has given me a word for you. I'll simply pass it on to you for whatever you hear in it: 'It is as you believe.'" Then he explained that he didn't wish to appear pious, but he felt that he would have been unfaithful not to share what had been given him. I had an ecstatic moment in response to those words, because they referred to my very purpose in writing this manual. Daniel had heard me say that I thought the Lord was calling lay men and women to significant ministries. "It is as you believe." When he received this revelation, wasn't it an ecstatic moment for Daniel as well as for me?

From the earliest days of the church, the people of God have sought to recognize and respond to the call of God. Sometimes they spent nights in prayer; sometimes they fled to the desert to live in caves and communes. Later they built monasteries, which were houses of prayer and discernment. Sensitive souls from Ignatius to Augustine have written rules of discernment to help all of us in our journeys. And today, in the twenty-first century, we are once again seeking ways to discern God's call and follow his direction.

In all our praying and searching and setting forth guidelines for discernment, let us never forget that discernment is not certitude; it is understanding according to the best of our ability. True discernment always leaves room for faith. Certitude doesn't require faith, and God is always desirous of faith. Our discernment points the way, suggesting how we should decide and act, but we act in faith, not certitude. God gives no guarantees about the outcome of our discernment, but he will be with us on our journeys and will teach us through our mistaken turns. And his divine fingerprints will mark our lives.

In matters of discerning God's direction in my life, I am always comforted by the confession of Thomas Merton, the well-known Trappist monk who wrote eloquently and honestly about his faith and life. No doubt I've used this quotation regarding discernment in another context. But it is so appropriate here that I can't resist quoting it again:

My Lord God,

I have no idea where I am going. I do not see the road ahead of me. I cannot know for certain where it will end. Nor do I really know myself, and the fact that I think that I am following your will does not mean that I am actually doing so. But I believe that the desire to please you does in fact please you.

And I hope I have that desire in all that I am doing. I hope that I will never do anything apart from that desire. And I know that if I do this, you will lead me by the right road though I may know nothing about it.

Therefore will I trust you always, though I may seem to be lost and in the shadow of death. I will not fear, for you are ever with me, and you will never leave me to face my perils alone.[2]

Exercises in Discernment

1. Write your own version of Merton's confession, describing what you think God may be calling you to do.
2. Test this notion by applying each of the signs of the Spirit of God discussed in this chapter. Think of each of these signs as a lens through which you can view the material of a call that you've excavated from your life experience. All of these signs probably won't figure into your call, but you will no doubt find more than one.

2. Merton, *Thoughts in Solitude* (New York: Farrar, Straus & Giroux, 1976).

3. Answer the following questions with respect to your call:
   - What degree of clarity do you feel about your call?
   - Does this call persist in your mind? Or can you easily forget about it?
   - Do you have a sense that this call is getting stronger or weaker?
   - Do you feel that there is a congruence of call and circumstance in your life?
   - What events have converged to bring this call to focus in your mind? Make a list of the various factors that contribute to your sense of call.
   - How would you describe the depth of your conviction about this call of God in your life?
   - In the moments when you say "yes" to this sense of call, does it bring peace to your soul?
   - Have there been ecstatic moments related to your call? For example, when you think about responding to this call, do you feel passion, jubilation, a powerful sense of commitment?
4. When you've written your honest answers to these questions, pause a few moments in prayerful silence.

CHAPTER FIVE

Wrestling with God — and Ourselves

The call of God often creates tension in our souls. For many of us, the tension becomes a struggle with God that often includes even more of ourselves — old perceptions, unresolved conflicts, and unanswered questions. In our contending with God, we also face personal conflicts as we deal with past successes and failures, our attachments to our possessions and our lifestyle, and our fears about the consequences of yielding to God. But when we stop to think about humans contending with God, we're struck by what a foolish contest it is! Job must have felt the foolishness of the struggle when God inquired, "Shall a fault-finder contend with the Almighty? Anyone who argues with God must respond" (Job 40:1-2).

The very notion of a human struggling with God brings to my mind Jacob's wrestling with the Almighty. After years of successfully managing his uncle's herds and "mooching" along the way, Jacob decided to return to Canaan. After saying good-bye to his uncle, he gathered up his family, his servants, his possessions (and a little bit more than was his) and departed for his home country.

As he neared his destination, his servants reported that his brother Esau was on the way to meet him. Jacob, terrified because he had stolen his brother's privileged place in the family, prepared an offering to appease Esau's wrath. He needed only a quick memory scan to locate the fear he had felt when he had left home to escape his brother's wrath. This fear may have fed on his more recent cheating and greed: during the breeding season, he had given special attention to his own cattle, goats, and sheep and had neglected his uncle's interests. Jacob had reason to be afraid.

Before the fateful day of meeting, Jacob sent Esau gifts from his herds. His servants spaced the gifts just far enough apart so that Esau received one peace offering after another. As another protective measure, Jacob divided his remaining estate into two camps. That way, if Esau attacked him and won, he wouldn't lose everything.

After making all these elaborate preparations, Jacob took his immediate family and crossed over the Jabbok River for the night. The story in Genesis continues, "Jacob was left alone; and a man wrestled with him until daybreak" (32:24). If we had only this statement describing the struggle, we might think this man was one of Esau's soldiers or one of Jacob's own servants — or perhaps represented Jacob's struggling with an internal conflict. But these speculations would miss the mark. Jacob was wrestling with a transcendent figure, either an angel or the Almighty. He struggled with the heavenly visitor until the sun was coming up. Then the transcendent figure cried out, "Let me go, for the day is breaking." But Jacob responded, "I will not let you go, unless you bless me."

The transcendent figure asked, "What is your name?"

"Jacob," he responded.

Then the figure declared, "You shall no longer be called Jacob, but Israel, for you have striven with God and with humans, and have prevailed." And he blessed Jacob.

This brief narrative depicts a man who had been called by God to possess the land that had been given to his grandfather, Abraham. He was compelled to respond to the call, but the call awakened his memories and unleashed his fears. He felt not only fearful of his brother but guilty before God. He felt inadequate for the task and fearful of the outcome. This struggle drove him to prayer, which is symbolized in his night of wrestling with the figure who eventually blessed him.

Just how many times has this dramatic struggle been played out in the lives of God's people? Jacob prevailed — not by overturning God's plan but by getting himself aligned with it. The blessing was indeed the *shalom* of God, and in numerous ways Jacob's paradigmatic experience informs our own struggle with the call of God.

In earlier chapters I introduced four individuals to you in some detail; each had felt the call of God. One man wondered if he was called to ordained ministry; another wondered if he was called to found a Bible institute. One woman was called to minister to the dying; another was called to rescue abused children. As you recall, none of these individuals found it easy to respond to the call. Rather, each felt somewhat conflicted about the call and how they should respond to it.

Another Jacob by Another River

I met Jay in Berkeley. During the early days of the class I was teaching in the summer school at the Graduate Theological Union, I noticed the searching eyes and hungry heart of this man. During the break on the second day, I made a point of seeking him out and engaging him in conversation. He was a most interesting individual.

Jay was an employee of the state, in charge of computer training for a department with three thousand employees. He managed a unit of twelve trainers that traveled throughout the state, introducing employees to a new statewide computer system. He liked his work and had advanced quickly.

But there was more to Jay than mere training and professional success. He was also a seeker. He and his wife had been members of the Presbyterian church in their hometown for a number of years. They were not only regular attendees but also hard workers. They taught in the educational program of the church and participated in the missionary outreach of the congregation. When Jay and I talked, the matter that quickly came to the surface related to his personal searching, not to his religious involvement in the church. Here was a man who was hard after God. Or perhaps a better way of describing his situation would be to say that God was hard after him.

The idea of this "double searching" often throws us into a quandary. Are we seeking God? Or is God seeking us? (We will discuss these questions more thoroughly as the chapter unfolds.) At any rate, the search was seriously underway in Jay's life. He was not only active in his congregation, but he was also attending various retreats and classes, like the one I was teaching. I found his evaluation of himself to be clear and honest. He knew there was a deeper dimension to faith than he was experiencing.

In the course of our conversation, I described the Certificate in Spiritual Formation that we offered at Columbia Theological Seminary. He seemed very interested in it, and I invited him to consider the introductory course that all participants take. That fall he responded to my invitation and came to what we call "Immersion Week." I think I can safely say that his wrestling at the Jabbok River had begun in earnest at this point. In a metaphorical way he could testify with Jacob about naming the place Peniel: "For I have seen God face to face, and yet my life is preserved" (Gen. 32:30). The struggle of this week was but an introduction to other struggles that Jay would face over the next few years.

Jay's first struggle began when he realized that his wife, Millie, hadn't shared in this Jabbok experience. He wondered how she could come to understand it if she hadn't experienced it. At the time I met him in Berkeley, Millie, although active in the church, didn't seem to be searching beyond her present experience. Would this transformation that Jay was beginning to experience alienate him from her? Does God engage in that sort of activity?

Over the next year, Jay participated in two or three more classes in the program at Columbia. God worked with him in significant ways concerning his lifestyle and values, and Jay began to make changes in how he conducted his life. He also faced issues in his vocation. Did his current job make wise use of his gifts?

In the second year of Jay's program at Columbia, Millie, at Jay's urging, attended a course taught by Walter Brueggemann. He referred to the same authorities that informed the anthropology courses she taught at a local college. Like most people, she was immediately inspired and challenged by Brueggemann's breadth of knowledge and his inimitable manner of presenting it. Because of her experience in this first course, she registered for the next Immersion Week and plunged headlong into the program, searching for God's will for her.

About the time that Jay was finishing the program, his job was becoming a critical issue for him. He had always enjoyed his work and felt that it was worthwhile both for the people he worked with and for the public at large. His issue wasn't so much with the work itself but with management's desire to promote him.

For the first time in his career, Jay engaged this issue in the light of his faith, his new sense of meaning and God's intention for him. Now, instead of asking what was best for him financially, he was asking, "What does God want from me?" It was this new perspective that created the tension. And he couldn't discover the answer without another struggle by the Jabbok River.

Jay was highly respected by his employees, and he was often praised by management as a model supervisor. In the end, he accepted a temporary promotion to try out the new position. But at the end of three months, he realized that his new job demanded so much of him that there was no time left for God. To continue on this course would mean putting in long days, always being on call, maintaining a frantic pace, and dealing with significant stress. It would mean using people as an expendable resource to be burned out and then tossed aside. It would mean "playing hard" to overcome the stress of "working hard." It would mean no time or heart for church activities or a spiritual life. In this wrestling with God, Jay ultimately found the courage to reject the promotion.

After he returned to his old job — not as demanding as the new job would have been, but still very hectic — Jay made an effort to slow down the pace of his life. But he still found himself too busy. He struggled with a calendar of five meetings a day, which left him no time to coach employees (his real job). The words "Trust me . . . trust me" kept arising in his prayers. One day the full answer came to Jay unexpectedly. The struggle at the Jabbok River was over. Jay requested a voluntary demotion and received it. He captured the insight he had been given in a poem of surrender entitled "I Am Learning":

I Am Learning

Loving God, I am learning to value being — to value who I am and whose I am. I am not what I do for a living, or what I have achieved, for all that is vanity. Instead, I serve the living, loving God — you — very ground of my being.

I am learning to serve — to yield my right to command and demand. In love I encourage others to be. I give up my need to manage and control.

I am learning to give up — my ego, so I may be a conduit through which you use my hands and feet to do your will on earth as it is in heaven.

I am learning your will — in daily choices that oscillate between idols of security versus risks of faith. I awake each morning and decide whether to continue the faith journey or settle for security. Your will is really about trust.

I am learning to trust — trust you to be God. Trust you to be in control, keep your promises, wish the best for me — trust you to love me. When I am unable to feel your presence, in prayer I dance slowly through the darkness.

I am learning to pray — to ask graciously for myself as well as others. The more I pray, the more I listen. In silence you speak your word that has no beginning or end. Slow be the pace.

I am learning to listen — with ears of the heart — learning to feel rhythms — act, pray, love, pray. Quietly flows the hymn of the universe — the sway of divine breathings. Surrender to the rhythm of redeeming grace.

Jay now works for one of his previous employees as a member of her team. He is very happy and fully engaged in his life with God.

Jay was strengthened as he faithfully worked his way through these struggles and discovered that the One who had called him was faithful. God revealed himself to Jay, guided him in his family relationships, helped him evaluate his job and his lifestyle, and showed him the source of his strength. Before offering you a deeper insight into this readily available source, I invite you to examine your own struggles more closely.

Are We Wrestling with God — or with Ourselves?

When the call of God presses heavily upon you and you sense you should make a decision, what do you say to yourself? What responses to God come most naturally to you? Do you feel you don't have the time to follow the call? Or do you have feelings of inadequacy or unworthiness? Do fears keep you from responding, or is there a family issue to which you retreat? This is a double-sided question. On the one hand it seems like you're wrestling with God, but on the other hand it seems like you're struggling with yourself. Perhaps it is both at once, as it was in Jacob's situation. A few prods may help you recollect your usual stumbling blocks (and excuses) when it's time for you to make a decision.

1. Do you feel too busy to respond to a call? Do you claim that you have so much to do that there's no time or space left over for God? No doubt most of us are really busy — overscheduled, overcommitted, and overworked. Our calendars have so many engagements on them every day that we neglect God, church, family, and ourselves. Our lives have become so programmed that when we hit "enter" on our life computer, our structured day begins automatically.

A while back I received an e-mail from a woman who was seeking spiritual guidance. Her minister had recommended that she contact me. Because we had met earlier, during a retreat I conducted for her church, she felt free to share with me her feelings of being trapped on a roller coaster of activity. The first thing I asked her to do was telephone me so that we could talk. During the course of our conversation, I suggested that she might get a grip on her life by doing a journaling exercise. I asked her to begin by answering a single question honestly and thoughtfully: "What's going on in my life?" This is what she wrote:

> In my external world, my life is chaotic — working 60 to 80 hours each week, being a wife, a mother, a coach for my daughter's Odyssey of the Mind team, a member of the personnel committee at church, etc. People keep asking me how I keep it all together. The truth is I don't hold my life together very well. I'm the daughter of a perfectionistic father and a mother with a martyr

complex — plus I'm driven by an unhealthy, extreme Puritan work ethic.

I don't do leisure well. I marvel at my husband's ability to just shut everything out and crash in the middle of the day to watch TV, read, or take a nap. Why can't I do the same? Seems like there's always a long list of things that need attending (laundry, dishes, picking up the house, mending our clothes).

Where's the time for me? Where's the time for God? I remember my minister once saying that there's a difference between "doing" and "being." My life is an awful lot of "doing" without a corresponding "being." Focusing on "being" is simply not in my nature. Is finding a way through this "packed-out" life possibly finding my way to God?

If this successful woman said, "I'm too busy," who would disagree with her? If God should call her to a special ministry, she would most likely answer, "I'm too busy." I suspect her response would be accurate, but she might be going so fast that she wouldn't even hear the call.

Perhaps for this wonderful, successful, and highly engaged person, the call of God would be a powerful interruption in a tightly structured, highly overworked life. I do understand this kind of life. I could have written a similar description just a few years ago. What about you? Does busyness keep you from responding to God's call?

2. Do you have feelings of unworthiness? I've talked with more than one person who, when called by God, felt so totally unworthy that their will was paralyzed. It's hard to blame anyone for this response. Who, after all, feels worthy of being addressed by God? A moment's reflection provides all the time we need to become aware that our hands aren't clean and our record isn't pure — but this God keeps calling us in spite of our imperfections.

I once spoke with a woman named Kayron who seemed particularly burdened by a sense of unworthiness. She had been raised in a Catholic home, but as a young adult she left the church. As the years went by, she married and divorced several times. Her sense of self-worth and self-confidence was completely eroded by these experiences.

Then she married a man who was stable and dependable — and, best of all, he loved her. In this loving relationship he prayed for her and encouraged her to worship with him. Fortunately, they chose a church with a minister who spoke clearly about God's love, and the congregation opened its arms to them as a couple. Both of them became genuinely active in the work of the church. So it seemed her life had been renewed in many ways.

When I spoke with her about her call, she at first responded enthusiastically: "Oh yes, I do believe that God has something for me to do!" Then she began describing her desire to help sexually abused children.

But after a few minutes she stopped talking. In the silence that followed, she bowed her head as if in prayer. Then in words barely audible she said, "But I feel so unworthy of God's call."

It was clear to me that although her present life circumstances were good, she was still haunted by her past. "Please don't let your past burden you," I encouraged her. "God has forgiven you for all your past mistakes — and our God doesn't nag us about our failures and inadequacies."

When Peter fell at Jesus' knees and confessed his unworthiness, Jesus didn't honor his confession by confirming it; instead he said, "Follow me." Perhaps this suggests that Jesus doesn't see us as unworthy.

3. Do you have feelings of inadequacy, a sense of unpreparedness? The mention of inadequacy brings to mind the exchange between Moses and the Most High God in Exodus 3:9-14:

> "The cry of the Israelites has now come to me; I have also seen how the Egyptians oppress them. So come, I will send you to Pharaoh to bring my people, the Israelites, out of Egypt." But Moses said to God, "Who am I that I should go to Pharaoh, and bring the Israelites out of Egypt?" He said, "I will be with you; and this shall be the sign for you that it is I who sent you: when you have brought the people out of Egypt, you shall worship God on this mountain." But Moses said to God, "If I come to the Israelites and say to them, 'The God of your ancestors has sent me to you,' and they ask me, 'What is his name?' what shall I say to

them?" God said to Moses, "I AM WHO I AM." He said further, "Thus you shall say to the Israelites, 'I AM has sent me to you.'"

Moses felt what any of us would have felt in the face of the challenge to deliver God's people from Egypt. "Who am I," asked Moses, "that I should go to Pharaoh and challenge him?" Moses had no army. He had no political connections in Pharaoh's court. The Israelites were too poor and powerless to mount an insurrection. Where could Moses turn?

In response to Moses' paralysis, the Lord said, "I will be with you." Shouldn't this be enough for Moses — and for us? But the Lord continued, "This shall be a sign for you that it is I who sent you: when you have brought the people out of Egypt, you shall worship God on this mountain." This declaration is no afterthought. It is not an addendum to the promise of presence; it is a sign that will underscore that presence. To paraphrase this promise, I would say, "Moses, when you bring the people out of Egypt and you stand alone at the peak of this mountain receiving my law and worshipping me, you will be reminded that I made the promise and fulfilled it." When Moses looked at the evidence, he would know that the God whose name is I AM WHO I AM (or "I will do what I will do") had delivered the people from bondage.

Although our call would never be on the same scale or level as the call to Moses, it could still be daunting enough to evoke feelings of inadequacy. Whatever God may call us to do, it is always a larger task than we can accomplish with our own strength. The call generally requires change, and with change comes risk, and risk raises our fears. When this train of responses reaches fear, we feel overwhelmed, and we must face our sense of inadequacy.

In all frankness, I doubt that any servant of God has felt adequate to the call. Most of us who have heard God's call have had to learn to depend on God and God alone. God promises always to be with those whom he calls. We can depend upon his presence to guide us when we don't know the way, to empower us when we're overcome with our feelings of inadequacy, and to manifest his will through us when we walk with him.

Over time I have become more intimately acquainted with some of the truly great leaders in the church, and I've discovered that they have the same feelings of anxiety and inadequacy that I do. On the outside they appear calm and full of confidence, but on the inside they experience their own inability to do the ministry of God without his help. Whether we're teaching God's truth, showing God's compassion to the poor, or working for justice, it's always the same. We simply can't do God's work apart from God's presence and help.

I remember the Sunday morning that I found myself in a pew in a West Coast church, listening to the confession of a dynamic young minister. He explained that earlier in his life he had felt called by God to preach, but that he hadn't felt released to the call. The word "released" fascinated me, and I wondered what he meant by it. Then came his explanation: When he had considered becoming a minister of the gospel, he had been overcome with feelings of inadequacy and weakness. "How could God use a person like me?" he had asked. He had found the answer in the text from which he was preaching that Sunday: Paul's first letter to the Corinthian church, in which he wrote,

> When I came to you, brothers and sisters, I did not come proclaiming the mystery of God to you in lofty words or wisdom. For I decided to know nothing among you except Jesus Christ, and him crucified. And I came to you in weakness and in fear and in much trembling. My speech and my proclamation were not with plausible words of wisdom, but with a demonstration of the Spirit and of power, so that your faith might rest not on human wisdom but on the power of God. (1 Cor. 2:1-5)

Could it be that our sense of inadequacy is always the prelude to receiving God's help?

4. Do you have a limited view of a call? Many people think that the only "called" people they know are ordained ministers. A friend of mine illustrates this misperception. God awakened her in the night, calling her name so that she couldn't sleep. In response, she consulted with her minister, she read the passages in Scripture about call, and she struggled with the notion of going to seminary.

75

Then the Voice spoke to her again: "My disciples in the early church did not go to seminary. They served me where they were with the gifts they had. You are called to serve me here with those gifts I have given you." A call from God doesn't necessarily mean that you should go to seminary or be in an ordained ministry. Be patient, listen, and wait for clarity in your call.

5. Does your marriage present an additional challenge? If you're married, your spouse's response to the call is always important. As a context for our discussion of the relationship of spouses when a call is heard, I turn to Paul's words to the Corinthian church. As you know, this church had many problems and issues, ranging from who should baptize whom, to whether or not to eat meat sacrificed to idols, to the question of the resurrection of Jesus. In this mixture of issues Paul also addressed the relationship of men and women. Because of the stresses of that particular time period, he seems to have advised against marriage (1 Cor. 7:8). But to those who were married he gave suggestions for maintaining the marriage (even though he himself was not married). He emphasized two matters of particular importance: first, that husbands and wives shouldn't deprive each other of sexual intercourse; and second, that each should live the life God called him or her to live (1 Cor. 7:1-7, 17).

From Paul's directives, two critical insights emerge. First, every person who is baptized into the body of Christ has a call from God, and it is important that he or she live out that call (1 Cor. 7:17; 12:4-13, 27). Few of us are wise enough or mature enough to discuss this issue before marriage, and so the call of God usually takes both partners by surprise. None of the people I talked with had anticipated a call from God, but all of them were highly sensitive to their spouses' sense of call. How would a wife respond to her husband's call to ordained ministry? How would a husband react to his wife's call to a healing ministry? What would it mean to a wife if her husband became a personal evangelist? Those with whom I have talked knew from the outset that moving slowly and talking through changes was a delicate but essential aspect of the call. It is painfully difficult for one person in a marriage to have an effective ministry until the call is properly negotiated.

Early in my marriage to Nan, the issue of spousal agreement became a critical issue for us. For four weeks the whole family had been with me during my final residency for the Doctor of Ministry degree at San Francisco Theological Seminary. With two weeks remaining, Nan and the kids returned to Atlanta, leaving me to do research for my doctoral project. During those two weeks I got deeply involved in studying environmental issues and in sensing a call to a change in lifestyle that related to my values.

As I was flying back to Atlanta, it struck me that Nan hadn't participated in the study and hadn't made the commitments I had regarding the issues. We hadn't even spoken about it in our daily phone conversations. Before the plane landed, I became increasingly anxious. I didn't bring up the issue during my first hours home, but Nan could tell from the look on my face and my behavior that something was making me tense. That night, as we shared a dinner out, she asked, "What's going on with you?"

I explained to her that I had been challenged to make some lifestyle changes regarding eating beef, using energy, and conserving resources. I then confessed that I was afraid that if I made the changes I felt called to make, it would seriously affect our relationship.

How fortunate I am. Nan listened patiently while I explained my fear of changing. When I finished telling her my feelings, she said very simply, "I love you and I'll support you in whatever changes you feel are necessary for us to make."

The Deeper Struggles

I don't want to minimize the fear, the pain, and the frustration that are part of our struggle with God's call. These responses and emotions are real, but they seem to be expressions of deeper inward struggles. I believe there are issues in our deeper selves that the call often evokes. For example, what are the deeper issues for the person who feels "too busy" to respond to God's call? What drives the calendar and the appointment schedule?

I suggest that we are driven people because of our social values and perceived personal needs. Why does the woman who spoke with me keep such a busy schedule? Why did I drive myself for years to take every speaking opportunity that presented itself to me? Every day, Western culture drives home the "importance" of the clothes we wear, the cars we drive, the homes we live in, and the outward trappings of success. Perhaps these values themselves have roots in our needs for security, recognition, and power. I believe that when we take a close look at our values and personal needs, we can find the roots of busyness. It seems to me that busyness is actually a symptom of a false value system or an impoverished ego.

I think our feelings of inadequacy often stem from a misguided imagination. Some of us have learned to see danger where danger doesn't exist; we've learned to fear the unknown because it might hold destructive powers. Both of these — a sense of danger and a fear of the unknown — are products of the imagination. Some of us can trace these feelings back to our formative years. We had mothers or other mentors who, in an effort to protect us from harm, constantly warned us about what *might* happen. In virtually all instances, the feared thing never did occur.

When I was growing up, my mother urged me to work hard and save my money because I never knew what kind of disaster might befall me. I did work hard and I did save my money, and for sixty years I've been waiting for that devastating thing to happen to me. I'm ready, but it hasn't come yet. A colleague of mine once said that I'd been running from poverty all my life, even though it hadn't gained a step on me in thirty years. Why did my mother say this to me? To make me a negative person? No — she was only trying to protect me from some of the difficult times she had lived through. She was orphaned at two, then lived with an uncle until she got out of college. Soon after she married, the country was plunged into the Great Depression, and she had a son in the midst of those very difficult years. Life had taught her to be prepared for hard times. Perhaps this piece of my life explains my compulsive workaholism. I suspect that all of us have stories that reveal these hidden fears.

A healthy imagination could create just the opposite picture of the future. If we were to see ourselves in partnership with God to accomplish his mission in the world, wouldn't that make a difference in our feelings? If we've been given gifts to implement the call that we've received, do we need to concern ourselves with weakness? The power for service comes not from us but from God.

To purge our minds of the unhealthy practice of imagining ourselves to be inferior or inadequate for the tasks to which we are called requires discipline. It may be that for years we've accepted the notion that if we can't always do things that are right and good, we can't live lives pleasing to God. Old ideas like this one must be challenged, resisted, and uprooted to permit the truth to shine into our imagination.

A negative self-image provides fertile ground for fears and doubts to grow. Never forget that we are created in the image of God! Of all God's creatures, we are those who can recognize God's glory and offer him praise. A frequent reading of Psalm 8 offers a healthy prescription for a negative self-image:

> O Lord, our Sovereign, how majestic is your name in all the earth!
>
> You have set your glory above the heavens. Out of the mouths of babes and infants you have founded a bulwark because of your foes, to silence the enemy and the avenger.
>
> When I look at your heavens, the work of your fingers, the moon and the stars that you have established; what are human beings that you are mindful of them, mortals that you care for them?
>
> Yet you have made them a little lower than God, and crowned them with glory and honor. You have given them dominion over the works of your hands; you have put all things under their feet, all sheep and oxen, and also the beasts of the field, the birds of the air, and the fish of the sea, whatever passes along the paths of the seas.
>
> O Lord, our Sovereign, how majestic is your name in all the earth!

The opening verses of Psalm 9 seem to be an appropriate response to the affirmations of Psalm 8:

> I will give thanks to the LORD with my whole heart; I will tell of
> all your wonderful deeds. I will be glad and exult in you; I will sing
> praise to your name, O Most High. (Ps. 9:1-2)

The affirmations of human beings in Psalm 8 are perhaps the most ex-
travagant to be found in Holy Scripture. The psalmist could only respond with the gratitude we see in the following psalm.

But self-image isn't the only issue. A further issue may be the source
of numerous fears we have about our call — the way we imagine God.
How do you think of God in relation to yourself?

Too many of us were raised in a religious environment that provided us with numerous reasons to fear God and to imagine that God
is the Sovereign to be placated lest we be destroyed. This negative view
of God inspired images of him as a judge or a policeman or a detective
rather than a loving, father-like or mother-like being who loved us,
nurtured us, and supported us. This negative image of God provided
too much judgment and fear and not enough love and compassion.
While others spoke of God's love, we often felt God's rejection and
judgment.

What if God has made you in his image? What if God loves you despite your feelings of unworthiness? What if God has chosen to use im-
perfect humans to do his work in the world? And what if at this very moment God is seeking your cooperation with his intention for your life?

What if you could imagine a God like that!

I hope you will bravely search beneath your fears and misgivings
and thoughtfully examine the deep causes of your resistance to the work
of God in you. Be careful not to make superficial responses to matters of
eternal importance.

One Person's Meditation

I've related the early struggles that Jay endured as he listened for God's
call. I think the following meditation that he wrote five years later (and
which he graciously agreed to let me use here) reveals a great deal about

the resolution of those inner and outer battles. The meditation points all of us to the source of healing for our inner struggles.

The Host

In prayer, God is the host and we are the guests. Like a host, God seeks to encourage and facilitate the conversation. But like unruly children, we are often brash, loud, and insensitive to the host's gentle hospitality.

If our prayer life feels like we are talking to a brick wall, perhaps it is because the host is patiently and graciously waiting for us to stop talking — waiting a lifetime if necessary. When the ideas are foreign to us, when the process is boring or meaningless, when the quiet sitting is a waste of time, then we begin to realize how out of tune we are with the mind of God.

"Incline your ear, and come to me; listen, so that you may live" (Isa. 55:3).

"Be still, and know that I am God" (Ps. 46:10).

God speaks the language of silence. To hear, we must come to quiet and stillness — life values that shut out the clamor and hurry of daily din. We must listen with the ears of the heart and develop a sensitivity to divine breathings.

"I will instruct you and teach you the way you should go; I will counsel you with my eye upon you" (Ps. 32:8).

Prayer is a process — a journey of growth and change. Our coach and mentor in this journey is Jesus, through whom we come to the Father. It is Jesus who molds us, teaches us street urchins good table manners, prays in us, and lovingly carries us to the Father (who is love). In this He is my savior.

Where does this lead? To inner peace and certitude, beyond reason and analysis. It is mystery. We put on the armor of God to withstand the consumerism, competition, and hurry sickness of our culture — to purge the idols, including idols of security. While practicing the presence in daily activities, we live in two worlds — time and eternity. We find gentleness in strength, and strength in gentleness.

"Steadfast love surrounds those who trust in the the Lord" (Ps 32:10).

Where does this lead? To trust and surrender, which is like falling off a cliff and hanging limp in the arms of Jesus — trusting God to love me, trusting God to be God. It's about giving up control. We trust enough to follow the stirrings of the Spirit as we are directed in daily activities. Thus we are a channel through which the Spirit flows, using us as His hands and feet in the world — the instrument of His will. We trust in order to go where we do not know, and never will it be the same — He in me, and I in Him.

Where does this lead? To unceasing prayer while doing justice, healing brokenness and pain, extending hospitality, being gracious, building community, imitating Jesus — and all the while falling in love with God. Acting while praying, praying while acting.

"Blessed are the pure in heart, for they will see God" (Matt. 5:8).

Where does Jesus carry us? To an intimate relationship, union and communion with the Father, in unceasing prayer. As our host, Jesus prays in us, and the Spirit hears our sighs that are too deep for words, while we rest in silent adoration of Holiness. Prayer becomes life, and life becomes prayer.

With ears of the heart, I feel Love say, "Rest, my child, rest." I lie quietly in the lap of God, folded in His arms like a weaned child in accepted tenderness. My restless heart is home at last.

"Now it is enough for you just to be. Later we will walk in the cool of the garden."

Amen.

Exercises in Discernment

1. Perhaps you've decided to accept God's call. If you haven't made that decision yet, try to identify your resistance to the call. Which of the following seem to apply to you?

- Feeling too busy
- Feeling unworthy
- Feeling inadequate
- Having a conflict with your spouse or significant other
- (Other)

    Write a short paragraph describing your struggle.

2. Look more deeply into your struggle by answering the following questions in writing:

    a. How do your personal values and priorities conflict with your sense of call?

    b. What negative consequences do you imagine if you answer God's call?

    c. Does a negative self-image hinder your response to God? If it does, how can you change it?

    d. Do you believe God can provide all that you need to fulfill your calling? Compose a prayer asking for what you feel you need at this moment.

CHAPTER SIX

The People Connection:
Reflections from Others

W here does a person turn for help in discernment? Most individu- als turn to other people. The sixteenth-century mystic Ignatius of Loyola confessed that at the time of his conversion he had no one to help him. Because he had no one else to instruct him, the Lord himself taught him as a schoolteacher teaches a little child. During that brief pe- riod of divine instruction, Ignatius claims, he learned more than he did in all the remaining years of his life. But few of us receive such direct guidance from the Lord. Maybe we don't take the time for it; maybe we're not as discerning as Ignatius. But we can seek out friends and other people we respect to find the help we need. This is the next step in discernment of call.

Thus far in our search for clear discernment of a call, we've exam- ined the anatomy of a call, the contents of our memory, the signs of God's presence in our lives, and the inner struggle the call often pro- duces. No matter what the call may be, all serious disciples look for clar- ity and confirmation before making a decision. Both of these words are key here: *clarity* about the direction of the call, and *confirmation* in our hearts that we have heard rightly.

The call may have originated within us as a yearning or a desire to do a particular thing, or it may have come from without, a direction that felt al- most like a demand. In addition to the type of call that seems to engage us so intimately, there also may be calls from others to assist in a particular type of ministry. Only in retrospect do we recognize God's voice in the human voice that extended the invitation. Some of us may even have been engaged with a ministry for a long time without having recognized that we were responding to God's call. I suppose that from a utilitarian perspective, the matter of personal calling doesn't matter as long as the mission is being accomplished. But I would argue that to be clear about your vocation as a response to God adds a dimension of intentionality that focuses both you and your vocation on God. In the new church of the twenty-first century, clarity about God's presence and intention will hold a much higher priority than it did in the cultural church of the century just passed. What I'm suggesting is that the present cultural church will evolve into a new and more Christ-directed community as the new century unfolds.

In our attempts to clarify the call of God, numerous resources abound. If we wish to know more about a particular situation, both the library and the Internet offer us opportunities for extensive reading and research that will expand our understanding of the context and import of our call. Increased knowledge will offer us insights into the task, with all of its risks and possibilities. Many of the people I've spoken with have told me that these resources have directed them to numerous sources to better inform them about their call.

Scripture is also a primary resource for discerning our call. I've already told you how Bible study was central to Daniel's search for clarity in his call. Laboring over the text for long hours every evening until he had made his way through the whole Bible confirmed the work of God in his life. Certainly Scripture offers all of us a rich resource of examples, norms, and directions for discerning our call.

Another way of discernment may be more practical and better-suited to those individuals who want to think rationally about their call. Elizabeth Liebert, a friend of mine who teaches spiritual formation at San Francisco Theological Seminary, recommends a down-to-earth approach to discernment. She suggests taking the following steps:

1. Form a clear question for discernment. It is important to be as clear and specific as possible.

2. Pray with an eye turned toward God rather than the transient things of earth. Ask others to pray for you. Pray until you desire God's will more than your own.

3. Gather appropriate information about your issue. Gathering information from the library or the Internet requires practical skills. What issues are raised around the specific issue you're considering? Whom does it affect and how? What does Scripture have to say about your issue? What does the Christian community — past and present, near and far — say? What have you learned in your life that addresses this issue? What do other people and the culture around you say?

4. List the pros and cons of your issue and pray through them. Here the process of discernment goes beyond standard ways of analyzing data. As you bring these items before God in prayer, pay attention to how you feel about each one of them — uneasy, angry, full of distaste, apathetic, fearful, happy, or at peace.

5. Make the decision that seems best. Often at this stage of discernment, the choice has become obvious. If it hasn't, have the courage to make the decision that has the most evidence, both internal and external, in its favor.

6. Bring your decision back to God in prayer. This time, pray from the perspective of having made the decision. This way of prayer permits you to "live" into the decision and to discover how it fits your life in Christ.

7. Live with your decision for several days or weeks before acting on it. Living into the decision provides space for you to see how you really feel about it. Are you embracing the decision — or is it making you feel uneasy? Uneasiness is a signal for you to reconsider your choice.

8. Look for inner peace and freedom. The peace of God signals confirmation for you. Peace is one of the important dialects in the language of God. Ignatius of Loyola emphasized peace as a sign of God's presence and affirmation. By this I mean that when we've made a tentative decision and lay our choice before the Lord, a continued sense of peace becomes assurance of our decision.

9. Follow your call step-by-step. Don't expect to see the end from the beginning. Learn the ways of God and the assistance of God as you

go. Keep a sense of humor and a sense of trust. When your sense of humor is faltering, trust. When your trust is shaky, draw on your sense of humor.

Professor Liebert's approach is practical — but it isn't a mechanistic way of discernment. She offers us principles, not wooden steps. You may move through the steps in a sequence that's different from the one you see here. For example, you may receive your answer before you've reached the final steps. It's important to remember to stay attuned to God throughout the discernment process. Continue on your own journey, and trust the Spirit to guide you.

You can also perform an "as if" experiment to get a feeling for the consequences of a decision. "As if" suggests that you make a tentative decision and live with it for a few days or a few weeks as if it's the direction for your life. Clarity often comes by living into the decision. I suggest that you look for both clarity and peace as the confirming marks of the Spirit. You may also consider confusion, uncertainty, and anxiety as signs that the direction is wrong for you or that you should wait a while longer before making the decision.

The Discernment of Others

All of these possible approaches to discernment can be enormously helpful to the seeker after God's will, and I commend each of them to you. But in this chapter I've chosen to focus the primary attention on discernment through other people — because most of us, in fact, are helped by others. When I asked my golf partner how his call to a ministry with the homeless came about, he said, "It came to me through another person, which is how it always happens for me." Although this isn't the only way for us to hear the Voice of God, it is perhaps singularly the most significant way for many of us. So I want to look with you at the role that others play in your discernment process.

I've called this chapter "The People Connection" because I believe that other people do reflect their perceptions of our call, and in their perceptions we often hear the Voice of God. The very act of stating our sense of call to another person clarifies it for us. Hearing the feedback from others also enhances our understanding. I emphasize the "people connection" because turning to others is the most natural thing to do, and often the most fruitful as well.

When you're struggling with a call, or even when you've arrived at clarity about a call, I believe it would be beneficial for you to get together with your trusted friends on a one-to-one basis and share your perception of call with them. In addition to such one-on-one conversations, you may also find it helpful to talk with a small group of spiritually sensitive people, inviting them to pray with you about discernment. The Quakers have developed a special way of using the people connection that has been helpful to many of us. They call it a "clearness committee." In this situation, a group follows clearly defined guidelines to help an individual "get clear" on the call of God. Finally, the church itself should be part of the people connection. Those who have authority over us in the church should also confirm our call after we have received it and clarified it by connecting with friends, a small group, or a clearness committee. If we are called to a ministry within the church or expressive of the church, this requirement needs no elaboration. Even when our call leads beyond the church, however, we would do well to get the church's affirmation before launching into it.

Unfortunately, not all baptized believers or even ministers know how to receive a person who is struggling with a call. A friend of mine provides a sad example. When she had a sense of call, she went to her minister and shared her perception of it. As she described the visit to me, she said, "The minister looked at me as if I had five heads, dismissed me, and that was that." Be sure that the person you choose to speak with has a deep knowledge of the love of God and the divine way of working.

Reflections from a Friend

Nothing is more natural or more safe than speaking with a friend about the deep things of the heart. We have seen how Mary, the mother of Jesus, struggled with the words of the angel until they were clear to her.

Once they became clear, she yielded herself up to the Lord's service, and said as much to the angel. But soon after the angel's departure, Mary rushed into the hill country to speak with her cousin Elizabeth.

When she met Elizabeth, she told her everything — about the angel's visit, about her acceptance of the call, and about the miraculous conception. Why did she hasten to see Elizabeth? Why was she so eager to tell someone? I believe that Mary was seeking greater clarification of her call and the acceptance and affirmation of someone who loved her. Elizabeth gave her both when she said, "Blessed are you among women, and blessed is the fruit of your womb!" Just like Mary, we also need someone to affirm our good news and celebrate it with us.

When we open our hearts and share our struggles with a friend, we also seek clarification. But receiving the clarifying word from a friend isn't always easy.

A friend once came to me with a big question. "What do you think about my running for Moderator of the Church?" he asked.

"Well," I said, "can you handle it if you don't win?"

"Yes, I think so. But I sure hope I win."

I think my question was hard and unexpected. My friend hadn't considered losing — and he didn't want to lose. In fact, some individuals take loss very hard. I've seen more than one person shattered because they interpreted a loss as an indicator of their worth to God and to themselves. I knew my friend would find it difficult to lose — hence my question. Hard questions help our process of discernment.

Another good friend also came to visit with me when she was seeking discernment. She had graduated from seminary and served two different congregations for about eight years. In recent months she had studied group spiritual direction, an offering of the Certificate Program at Columbia.

She explained that she had resigned as pastor of her church. She had decided to leave because her vision for the church didn't match that of the congregation.

"Now," she said, "I have to discern what I'm going to do."

"What do you think your gifts are?" I asked her.

"I'm an entrepreneur," she responded. "I'm ecumenical, and I'd like to remain in the city where we live because of my connections with the people there. I have a seat on the Presbyterian Foundation Board, and that's important to me." She continued by telling me that she enjoyed creative worship and that she had a vision of training laypeople as servant leaders.

I listened to her elaboration of a vision for lay ministry. Then I asked her if she had ever thought about forming a house church — by which I meant gathering a small group of people (from a dozen to twenty) in a home for worship and prayer and ministry.

"Yes, I've thought about it."

"Then why not do it?" I inquired.

She was very honest in her response. She told me that she was anxious about the possibility of members from her former congregation joining the house church, and she also wondered if the governing body would permit it.

As we continued our conversation, it seemed to me that God was speaking to her through my questions and to me through her responses. In a person-to-person interchange, God speaks to us and through us. This mutuality characterizes the interaction of people who are discerning Godspeech.

I hope these two examples give you a picture of the natural, honest conversation that friends can have when they are discerning together. But you may still be wondering exactly what you should discuss in a discerning conversation with a friend.

When you meet with a friend to talk about your sense of call, begin by telling this person why you're speaking with him or her at this particular time. Let your friend know that this conversation isn't a casual matter to you. Be sure to explain how the sense of call came to you and what your struggles are. Listen carefully to the responses your friend gives, and pay close attention to the questions he or she asks. Explore these questions and honestly confess both your struggles and your fears. When you've finished the conversation, ask your friend to pray for you (if you feel comfortable enough to make that request).

Reflections from a Group

Dependence upon group consensus and group response in the process of discernment has long been a part of the Christian tradition. This approach to discernment reaches back to the earliest days of the church, when it was seeking a successor to Judas, electing deacons, and discovering exciting modes of worship. The approach has deep roots in Saint Paul's vision of the church as the Body of Christ. According to his vision, we are all baptized into one body and are members one of another with gifts to share with each other. The sharing builds up the Body of Christ and contributes to our common good. (See 1 Corinthians 12:4-7, 12-13, 27.)

After the ascension of Jesus, Peter declared to the other apostles that someone had to be chosen as a witness to Jesus' resurrection. The successor of Judas had to be someone who began with them at the time of John's baptism and continued with them until Jesus ascended. Two people who had these qualifications were nominated from the group. At that point Scripture says, "And they cast lots for them, and the lot fell on Matthias; and he was added to the eleven apostles" (Acts 1:26). Apparently the "casting of lots" method didn't achieve accurate discernment, because later Paul claimed that he was made an apostle by Jesus Christ, thus making himself one of the twelve (Gal. 1:1). This incident suggests that the early church understood and used the group principle, but it also indicates that not all decisions made were perfect ones.

In another instance, the work of the apostles became so demanding that they couldn't attend to all of the details involved. The Greeks complained that their widows weren't getting the same treatment as the Hebrews' widows. In the midst of this controversy, the apostles called the believing community together and said, "It is not right that we should neglect the word of God in order to wait on tables" (Acts 6:2). They asked the community to select worthy persons for the task of giving food and assistance to the needy. The suggestion pleased the community, and seven persons were chosen and ordained. (See Acts 6:1-6.)

In the Corinthian correspondence, Paul gives us a brief glimpse into group participation in the worship life of a congregation. He says,

"When you come together, each one has a hymn, a lesson, a revelation, a tongue, or an interpretation. Let all things be done for building up" (1 Cor. 14:26b). Although this text focuses on worship and doesn't specifically mention discernment, it nevertheless illustrates the "body principle." Each person in a group brings to it a gift that is valuable for building up other members.

Why is a small group a good place to receive the reflection of the community? Because the group is united in Christ. Because they've been baptized into his body and made members of each other. Because they feel each other's pain and share each other's woes. Where on earth could you find a better place to seek discernment?

In addition to being grounded in Christ, each member of the group brings a special gift — whether it be the gift of faith, of support, of discernment, or of administration. Like the gifted persons in worship, these gifted individuals know the right questions to ask, and they have insights to share.

The small group also provides a setting in which creative interchange takes place. The word from one person sparks an insight in another. That individual shares his or her insight, and so it goes. As the Spirit works in all the members of the group, it receives greater clarity.

The small group not only helps discern the gift and the calling in a fellow member; it also offers support for the ministry. In this respect the group provides a better setting for discernment than a one-on-one encounter because often the group not only discerns but also helps engage the task.

At a recent birthday celebration, I was talking to the honoree's son-in-law. This young physician began telling me about his sixty-hour workweek and how it sucked all the energy right out of him. In the midst of our conversation he began to talk about the nine people — including his mother, his father-in-law, and me — who had shared birthdays with each other for over twenty years. This meant nine meals together every year — and extra time spent together on snow days, holidays, and sometimes just ordinary days. The son-in-law commented, "You love each other, you're there for each other, you can call on each other for anything — and this has been going on for twenty years."

Then he began to say, "This is what . . ."

" . . . the church ought to be." I finished his sentence.

The members of our group, who originally began meeting to share birthday celebrations, have become a family, a group of believing people almost like a church. Perhaps that's why one of our members felt free to share a deep struggle going on in her family. And maybe caring about her, being there for her, and loving her provided the context in which she could seek direction from a trusted group.

Reflections from the Church

The church as a gathered community has always served as a resource for discernment. Like the small group, the larger assembly offers the benefit of all the gifts of the people of God, but the church also possesses God's administrative authority. This body offers discernment on many levels, from matters of local import to matters of international import.

Already we have seen how the apostles brought the church together to discern a matter of local missions. Then the church, in a corporate discernment of mission, called seven members to be deacons who would provide food and assistance to the Greek widows. These seven were ordained and empowered by the church for this task.

In the early days of the church, another incident called for discernment regarding a larger and more significant matter. Paul and Barnabas had completed the first missionary journey, proclaiming the message not only to the Jews but also to the Gentiles. After many Gentiles were converted to the faith, teachers from Jerusalem demanded that they be circumcised to fulfill the law of Moses. This requirement flatly contradicted the message that Paul and Barnabas had proclaimed. The matter couldn't be resolved locally, so a council of the whole church was called to hear the case in Jerusalem.

After hearing testimony on both sides of the matter, the church listened for God to speak. After they prayerfully considered the issues that were at stake, James was given a word of wisdom that affirmed the ministry of Paul and Barnabas and the freedom of the Gentiles from the law of Moses.

When the council ended, the church sent a letter to the Gentile Christians stating the result of their corporate discernment:

> "The brothers, both the apostles and the elders, to the believers of Gentile origin in Antioch and Syria and Cilicia, greetings. Since we have heard that certain persons who have gone out from us, though with no instructions from us, have said things to disturb you and have unsettled your minds, we have decided unanimously to choose representatives and send them to you, along with our beloved Barnabas and Paul, who have risked their lives for the sake of our Lord Jesus Christ. We have therefore sent Judas and Silas, who themselves will tell you the same things by word of mouth. For it has seemed good to the Holy Spirit and to us to impose on you no further burden than these essentials: that you abstain from what has been sacrificed to idols and from blood and from what is strangled and from fornication. If you keep yourselves from these, you will do well. Farewell." (Acts 15:23-29)

When the Gentile congregations heard this word, they rejoiced. Although this directive sounds strange in a modern context, it is important to remember that the council's ruling freed these early Christians from the Jewish ceremonial law and focused them upon Christ.

The decision by the Jerusalem council not only affected these new Christians but also legitimated the calling of Paul. At the time of his conversion, the Spirit testified to Ananias that Paul would take the message of Christ to the Gentiles. At the conclusion of his first missionary journey, the church council gathered in Jerusalem confirmed his ministry.

This original assembly in Jerusalem prefigured a long succession of church councils in which major doctrinal and ethical issues were settled. This first council also modeled the role of denominational gatherings and local church governing bodies that must make critical decisions for the church today. For example, if a person feels called to be a missionary in Jamaica or Haiti, that individual must receive approval from the missionary agency of the church.

When I was in college, one of my older classmates decided that God had called him to serve as a missionary in Korea. He gave witness to his call, raised funds, and purchased supplies for his sojourn. But after he sailed all the way to Korea, the authorities wouldn't permit him to disembark. His only option was to return home and confess his failure. Independent decisions like this one — well-intentioned though they might be — threaten the church's integrity and frustrate the plan of God.

Laura's story provides a contrasting example. Although she had been raised in the church, she turned away from it as a young adult. She devoted most of her time to developing her golf game, and she won a number of amateur tournaments. But along the way she made mistakes that created an abundance of self-doubt. After several years of struggle, she decided to seek God's help.

God came into her life with gracious forgiveness and acceptance, and he called her to be an evangelist. Today Laura radiates the love of God. I've never met someone who manifests the gifts of an evangelist the way she does. Her style is imaginative, her approach is gentle, and the results of her witness are quite amazing.

She is bold and imaginative in the ways she reaches out to others. After seeing the ad "Got Milk?" she had a large sign printed for the van she drove that read "Got God?" Even though she ran a business with her husband, she wasn't too busy to talk with a single mother who worked in the business and help her to Christ.

Next Laura hit on the idea of giving away bottled water to the walkers who exercised daily at a popular track in her area. She bought the water, then had wrappers printed up for the bottles that offered the "Water of Life" at her church. She thought this was a good mode of outreach. But no one in the church had given her permission to advertise the church in this fashion. Since this was a class-conscious congregation, some of its members thought this approach was a bit lowbrow.

Unfazed, Laura asked the governing body of the church for direction. They asked her to remove the name of the church from the label.

She did as they asked, but still continued her ministry of giving water to dozens of walkers at the track.

Whether the response of some of the members was correct is a matter for debate. What cannot be debated is Laura's call as an evangelist and her willing submission to the authority of the church. Her authenticity is underscored not only by her success in her work but also by her willingness to yield to authority.

It is wise for all of us to seek authority and legitimacy for our call through the larger gathering of the church. I'm sure there are some individuals who have been called by God and sent by him without the affirmation of a congregation. And their work for the kingdom may be highly effective. In most instances, however, it is best to have the backing of the Body of Christ for our efforts in ministry.

Reflections from an Intentional Group

Those of us who are seeking discernment of a call owe a debt of gratitude to the Quakers for developing the clearness committee as a way of gaining discernment. I had never heard the term until about ten years ago, when a friend of mine needed new direction in his life. My work had kept me in contact with Hal for over twenty-five years. He had directed a nonprofit lay ministry in Chicago for most of those years, and the time had come for him to move from that stage of his life into the next one. Hal was faced with the question many of us have faced: "What is God calling me to do now?"

When I was visiting Hal on one of my trips to Chicago, I asked him how he was going to determine his new direction. He told me, "I've selected a clearness committee, and they're meeting with me on Sunday evening." That was the first time I'd heard of such a group — but Hal didn't give me very many details about exactly what it was or how it worked.

Several years passed without the notion of a clearness committee crossing my mind. Then I was invited to participate in a conference at the Fetzer Center in Kalamazoo, Michigan. The leaders of the conference planned to introduce the participants to the idea of using a clearness committee as a way of discernment. And not only would we learn about what a clearness committee was; we would actually experience it.

The aim and the process of the experience were clearly defined for us. Four people attending the conference were chosen to seek guidance from clearness committees; then four clearness committees were formed with the remaining participants, with five or six people in each committee. (I was part of one.) Each "seeker" was first asked to write a two-to-three page paper describing the issue about which he or she needed discernment. The paper included not only the specific issue but enough of the background to help the committee members get a clear picture of the individual's circumstances. Because of the constraints of time and context at the conference, the committees didn't have an opportunity to actually read these papers before their meeting time. We were informed that each meeting would last no longer than two hours.

When my committee gathered, there were five of us plus the gentleman seeking discernment. We were told that as committee members we could only ask questions. The questions couldn't be leading questions or questions that disguised advice. Pure, straightforward questions were the order of the day. Because we hadn't had a chance to read the gentleman's statement, we took a few minutes at the beginning so that he could describe his circumstances and the issue about which he needed discernment.

One member of the committee had been designated to start the proceedings, call us to silence, and gently correct us when we sought to give advice rather than ask a question. After we heard the presentation of the issue, she suggested that we enter into silence for ten minutes. Afterward she broke the silence with this question: "What question came to you out of the silence?" One committee member after another asked the gentleman a question. He could answer the question or choose not to answer it if he desired. After this first round of questions, the committee observed another period of silence, then asked more questions. This process continued for an hour and a half. Then the proceedings were brought to a close, and the gentleman thanked all of us for our help.

My description of the experience of a clearness committee may sound very ordinary, but I can tell you that the experience was anything but that. We all experienced the presence of the Spirit in an extraordinary way. I experienced the Spirit of God at work among the people in our group just as strongly as the Spirit seemed to be at work in the man we were questioning. I was struck by the frequency with which a committee member asked a question that was also on my mind. The depth of the questioning resists description; what happened can't be captured in words. With each entry into silence and the ensuing round of questions, the relationship deepened, and the committee became more of a community. It was amazing to see how each question seemed to take the man deeper and deeper into himself.

I don't know how all these things happened in that meeting, but I saw a gathering of strangers become a community. Even in what seemed like the relatively simple process of asking questions, people gave deeply of themselves. And the questions we asked often became questions about our own lives and callings. So I urge you not to be deceived by the seeming simplicity of a clearness committee.

Personal Discernment: The Final Word

While I've hinted at and sometimes described various options for clarifying our sense of call, in this chapter I've focused attention on one-on-one conversations, small-group wisdom and discernment, congregational discernment, and discernment via a clearness committee. These sources of help all demand face-to-face meetings. And they can be immensely valuable. Yet it is important to acknowledge that, while the reflections of others can be enormously helpful, the final decision rests in our hands. In the deep chambers of our soul where we meet the Holy God, we must make a decision and and take responsibility for it.

The stories and writings of Anthony de Mello have inspired me many times. He always seems to have a way of vividly symbolizing an issue and cutting right to the heart of a matter. In two succinct paragraphs he states the other side of the people connection. He gives testimony to the fact that at the end of the day, each of us must seek our answers from God and take responsibility for the decisions we make.

De Mello says to the Lord,

"I have, unfortunately, had a surfeit of people I could turn to for guidance. They badgered me with their persistent teachings till I could barely hear you through the din. It never occurred to me that I could get my knowledge firsthand from you, for they sometimes said to me, 'We are all the teachers you will ever have; he who listens to us, listens to him.'

"But I am wrong to blame them or to deplore their presence in my early life. It is I who am to blame. For I lacked the firmness to silence them; the courage to find out for myself; the patience to wait for your appointed time; and the trust that someday, somewhere, you would break your silence and reveal yourself to me."[1]

May you have the wisdom to seek guidance from others but the courage never to accept even their best guidance as the final answer. Press on beyond the words of friends and committees and church to hear the word of God for yourself.

Exercises in Discernment

Examining your resistance to God's call enables you to get "unstuck" and to move forward. At this stage of your engagement with the call, you need input from others to help you confirm the conclusion that you're coming to. Try the following exercises:

1. Choose a friend and discuss with him or her your sense of call and the struggle that you're having. After your conversation, write a short summary of it.
2. Select three or four friends and ask them to meet with you. At the start of your meeting, you might suggest that the group be silent together for three or four minutes. After the silence, tell them where you are in your call experience and ask for their response. Listen for

1. De Mello, *The Song of the Bird* (Garden City, N.Y.: Image Books, 1984), pp. 171-72.

God to speak through these individuals. Write a summary of what you hear from the group.

3. If you haven't done so already, talk to your minister about your call.

4. If your minister responds favorably to your call, ask him or her to set up a meeting with the governing body of the church. Share with them your sense of call, and ask for their guidance. Write a summary of their response.

5. Make a tentative decision based on your present clarity of call. Live with that tentative decision for a few days or a few weeks.

CHAPTER SEVEN

Discernment to Act

The final aim of discernment is not information or knowledge but action! Too frequently sincere people confuse information about God's calling or knowledge of the ways of God's working with the task of discernment. While it is true that both information and knowledge play essential roles in discernment, the final aim of discernment is obedience to God, making the intention of God concrete in history. In many ways this point seems too obvious to elaborate, but many serious disciples get "stuck" in the discernment process and never proceed to action.

What I call the "crystal-ball perversion" illustrates perfectly the problem of delayed obedience. In seeking to discern God's intention for us, we are often curious about the outcome of our obedience. We also wish to know what challenges and issues we will face along the pathway of fulfilling God's intention for us. We imagine that if we had all this information, we could make a better decision about following God's guidance. This desire for "pre-knowledge" is what I mean by the crystal-ball perversion: we want to look into the crystal ball and see the future to eliminate risk. But this alternative also eliminates trust. God doesn't provide crystal balls for curious disciples.

Discernment leads to action. In teaching courses in spiritual formation, I developed a number of exercises for students that helped them experience the skill or principle I was teaching. But in discernment there are no practice sessions. Engaging in discernment relates to you and to real issues in your life; there's no room for role-playing. Playing at discernment would be a farcical enterprise.

An Early Church Experience

To further explore this "go for broke" nature of discernment, let's look in on a worship/discernment experience in the Antioch church of the first century:

> Now in the church at Antioch there were prophets and teachers: Barnabas, Simeon who was called Niger, Lucius of Cyrene, Manaen (a member of the court of Herod the ruler), and Saul. While they were worshiping the Lord and fasting, the Holy Spirit said, "Set apart for me Barnabas and Saul for the work to which I have called them."
>
> Then after fasting and praying they laid their hands on them and sent them off. So, being sent out by the Holy Spirit, they went down to Seleucia; and from there they sailed to Cyprus. When they arrived at Salamis, they proclaimed the word of God in the synagogues of the Jews. (Acts 13:1-5)

This description of an informal worship service reveals many significant details and events, including the call of Paul and Barnabas, the birth of the missionary movement of the church, and the centrality of prayer in the life of the early congregations. But I call your attention to an event of striking importance. In the midst of worship, the Spirit spoke to the group: "Set apart for me Barnabas and Saul for the work to which I have called them."

The Spirit spoke, but the record elaborates neither how the Spirit spoke nor how those gathered discerned the call. Perhaps Simeon or Lucius heard the voice of the Spirit and gave utterance to the call before the group. Or perhaps Paul or Barnabas heard the call and spoke to the group, seeking their concurrence. Then again, the Spirit could have spoken in such a way that everyone present heard the Voice. Whatever conjectures we might make, we aren't privy to the ways of the Spirit that day. But we do have evidence that the small community knew that they had been addressed by God.

The discernment of the Spirit led to immediate action: "Then after fasting and praying they laid their hands on them and sent them off." When the community heard the call of the Spirit, they obeyed. Discernment led to action, to immediate action. Of what value is discernment if it doesn't lead us to prompt obedience?

That day in Antioch, something happened that exceeded both the understanding and the wildest expectations of the disciples. The disciples' response to the Spirit gave birth to the missionary outreach of that congregation. In fact, their discernment went far beyond that particular congregation: it gave birth to the missionary movement of the Christian church, an impulse in the community of faith that stretches from Antioch to Atlanta, and to your hometown as well. In the most dramatic way imaginable, the discernment of the Spirit led to specific, concrete action. And any so-called discernment that doesn't lead to action is a sham.

The New Epistemology: Doing in Order to Know

The new epistemology reverses the acts of knowing and doing. The usual way of taking action requires research, the accumulation of data, and a decision that leads to action. In this aspect of discernment, we discover what might be called the epistemology of Jesus: we act or obey in order to know. This principle, as we have seen, was illustrated in the church at Antioch. That small group of disciples had no way of knowing the outcome of their obedience. They prayed over Barnabas and Saul and sent them forth on the mission. First they obeyed, and then they knew. This principle finds further elaboration in one of Jesus' encounters with the Pharisees.

Late in his ministry Jesus attended the Festival of Booths, a celebration commemorating the years that the ancestors lived in tents while wandering in the wilderness. Because Jesus at first didn't make his presence known, many of the Jews were asking where he was. And the crowds were talking about him, some saying that he spoke truly of God, while others claimed that he deceived the people. At the midpoint of the festival, Jesus went up into the temple and began to teach. Then the Pharisees began to question his authority and authenticity. In response to the Pharisees' antagonism, Jesus said, "Anyone who resolves to do the will of God will know whether the teaching is from God or whether I am speaking on my own" (John 7:17). This is the new principle, doing in order to know. This statement explicitly makes doing the ground for knowing. We do the will of God to know the will of God.

Even when you've utilized all of the principles that we've explored regarding discernment of the Spirit, a dimension is missing until you act. In that space between rational understanding and completed discernment lies the act of doing. It is the act of doing that permits you to engage in making the will of God actual in the world. And many who are "followers of the way" testify that they see the hand of God in their lives much more clearly in retrospect than they did in prospect. This retrospective discernment suggests that before they acted they had no firm certainty that their discernment was correct, but after they obeyed, they were able to clearly see God's hand guiding and directing them.

All efforts to listen to the call of God, to scan our memories for clues, to look for signs of God's presence, to engage in the struggles with God and ourselves, and to listen to the reflections of others — all these efforts are wasted unless we act. Discernment is not heaping up information about God, and it is not primarily concerned with acquiring spiritual wisdom; it is about doing the will of God. In doing we arrive at knowing!

A Story of Doing

I first met Ronald while working in his church. As part of my work I set aside several hours each week for appointments with church members.

In most instances I talked with them about the call they were experiencing and how they might discern God's voice in it. One Wednesday afternoon, Ronald came in for a conversation.

When we sat down to talk, I noted a sense of heaviness about him. He had energy and spirit, but there was something weighing him down. I invited him to tell me about himself, and he proceeded to outline his life. He had been raised in the area and had attended school there. After serving in the Vietnam War, he returned home. Shortly thereafter he had an opportunity to work in California. While working on the West Coast, his life took a turn that led to great disappointment and pain, a pain that still lingered. Hearing the background of his life enabled me to listen more sensitively to his present sense of call.

The call with which he was struggling had crept up on him in a gradual, almost imperceptible way. He had been searching for a direction for his life but hadn't immediately found an answer. As it happened, his wife served as chair of a council on abused children. She asked Ronald to teach a course on parenting abused children that focused on the skills of listening and responding to clearly perceived messages. He developed the course and became quite good at teaching it. Numerous individuals told him how much it helped them not only in their relationship with their children but also in their relationship with their spouses.

The course Ronald taught, combined with his wife's work with at-risk children, brought him into contact with three alternative schools in the area. One of the schools was dedicated to mentally challenged children, another to children who were in trouble with the court; the third was a home for juvenile delinquents. The latter group was incarcerated and lived with numerous restrictions.

When Ronald visited these schools, he discovered groups of children who appeared fairly normal. They looked like they could have been from almost any school. But what didn't appear on the surface was the pain and abuse that marred their backgrounds. Nearly all of the children had been physically, emotionally, or sexually abused. Often their parents were alcoholics or drug addicts or both. As a result, these children had experienced a side of life that no child should have to endure. When Ronald talked with them, they said things like, "I wish I had someone to talk to," "I've gotten a rotten deal in life," and "What hope do I have for the future?"

Ronald heard these cries for help, and when he spoke with the school's leaders about providing some assistance, he found them more than eager to cooperate. This gave Ronald the courage to talk about a mission to these children first with his pastor, and then with the governing body of his congregation. He requested help from the pastor and permission from the governing board to create a committee that would seek ways to respond to these at-risk children. Permission was granted.

At the time Ronald and I talked, the committee had been meeting for about six months. They had done a great deal of talking and some praying, but they had made little progress in actually getting the ministry underway. Because of a prior conversation with the pastor, I already knew that Ronald was struggling with the call. When he got permission to form the committee, he thought that once he presented the idea, the committee would organize the ministry and get it launched. To his surprise, this didn't happen, although the committee's lack of initiative was predictable. In many of the committee meetings Ronald tried to detach himself from the work of organizing and administering the ministry by suggesting that they hire a director. It never became clear to me why Ronald wanted this detachment — whether it was because he felt inadequate to the task, was afraid of failing at it, felt too busy to undertake it, or felt unworthy of it. Whatver the reasons, both Ronald and the committee had been struggling for six months to begin a ministry that they all felt was essential.

The critical issue that Ronald wanted to talk about was the presentation he planned to give to the governing body of the church at a retreat scheduled to be held in two weeks. He wanted my input. I asked him to tell me his ideas, and after hearing them, I offered a few suggestions that he felt would improve his presentation. After laying out a way of engaging the other leaders in the church, I felt compelled to tell Ronald that this ministry was his vision and his call, and that it couldn't be delegated to a committee or to a hired worker. For very busy people with a corporate executive mentality, the trap of delegation is very easy to fall into. But it is critical to remember that the person pregnant with the vision must give birth to the vision! If God has called you to a ministry, you can't give it away. You may share it, but you can't delegate it. God called you, and you can't give the call away to a stand-in, a second, or a substitute.

Ronald needed more than a lecture about claiming his vision and responding to his call. He needed some help in structuring his presentation to the leaders. Below I've listed the suggestions that I offered him because, even though they're tailored somewhat to his situation, they're also appropriate for beginning a variety of ministries in the church:

> First, be clear in your focus. You want those who are listening to you to join with you in mentoring these at-risk children. Don't corrupt your central point by confusing your listeners with too much extraneous data. Keep the idea of mentorship clearly before them.
>
> Second, give witness to your call. Tell them how you got involved with this need, how you believe God spoke to you, and why you need help.
>
> Third, invite the leaders to gather into groups of five or six and discuss the need and their feelings about the children. At the close of the discussion, invite the whole group to become quiet and enter into a period of silence. Ask them one question: "Is God calling you to participate in this ministry?"
>
> Fourth, explain clearly and succinctly what you wish them to do. People find it difficult to answer a call if they don't have a clear picture of what's expected of them.
>
> Fifth, invite people to sign a commitment that indicates that they feel a call to the ministry or that they're open to exploring a call to this ministry. Write a personal note to each person who responds to the challenge.
>
> Sixth, start small. Form one group at a time, and work with them until they feel clear in their tasks and comfortable with their call.
>
> Seventh, after a month or so, call a meeting with those who have been engaged in the ministry to listen to their stories. This is

important! They need to talk about their experiences, you need to hear about them, and others in the group will benefit from hearing them too.

Eighth, begin calling the next ministry group.

Ronald took these suggestions and made an excellent presentation to the officials of the church. I sat in on his presentation to see how well it was received, and afterward I commended him on the fine job he did.

Far more people than he had expected signed on with the ministry. The leaders were enthusiastic about the opportunity and were willing to commit time and money to make it effective.

About six months after my initial conversation with Ronald, I decided to visit his church to see how the ministry was going. Surprisingly, I ran into him in the parking lot, and the difference I saw in him immediately caught my attention. He had a gleam in his eye, a smile that spread from ear to ear, and a lightness of spirit that bespoke a joyful state of soul. He told me that the ministry was going very well.

During my visit I sought to discover how others felt about the ministry to children at risk and how extensive the work was. My conversations yielded abundant information. The church had formed three groups that were ministering to the children. One group was serving as tutors, helping them with their schoolwork. Another was sending birthday cards and greeting cards to students they had chosen. Another group was visiting the children every week, seeking to befriend them. The results were gratifying.

One woman told me about serving as a mentor to a little boy of twelve. His teacher told her that he was constantly acting out his anger and frustration, but that when Beverly came to visit him, he seemed as normal as her own children. He was so grateful for her visit that he couldn't act out his negative feelings when she was present.

One little girl who had gotten a card from the "writing group" showed it to one of the mentors. She beamed with pride that someone had put her name on the card and written a special note to her. Such a small affirmation meant so much.

One group of women in the church adopted an entire class. They made an appointment to visit with the class while school was in session. During that time they asked the class to list some of the things they'd like help doing. The children made a verbal list: "Plant a tree." "Pick up trash." "Build a birdhouse." "Babysit." The women couldn't imagine their own children making such a simple list.

One of the men who was serving as a mentor took his golf clubs to show to his mentee. The twelve-year-old boy had never held a golf club in his hands before.

As one church member reflected on the ministry, she commented, "I'm awed that so little means so much to these children. We don't have to work and plan. We only have to be there."

Do you see how Ronald and the members of this congregation came to know the will of God by doing the will of God?

I've told this extended story not only because it has a strong focus on doing but also because it illustrates many of the issues surrounding the beginning of a ministry. In this story we see a call arising out of pain, which is so often the case. Ronald showed wisdom in talking with the pastor and the governing body of his church before going ahead with his ministry. Signs of the presence of God became clearer as the original group he was working with struggled together, developed plans, and invited others to share in the ministry. In this instance the person being called was engaged in the work before the call became clear to him. The response of the church leaders confirmed the validity of the call. After getting stuck, he sought me out as someone who could reflect with him on his call and figure out how to get it started. Struggles appear everywhere in this narrative: in Ronald's personal life, in the committee, and in the launching of the ministry. Confirmation of the call came after they began to do the ministry.

A Deeper Examination of Doing to Know

As I review the experience of Ronald in his call and the initiation of his ministry, it's obvious to me that he had to move beyond concern for the children and a bogged-down committee that focused on planning rather than acting. After a period of resisting the call by waiting for others to pick up on the vision, it became clear to Ronald that it was his call to fulfill. The church could have hired a full-time director, but that person wouldn't have had the vision. God called Ronald, and he had to answer the call with commitment.

Ronald had a choice in this situation. He could have elected to turn away from the pain of the children. He could have dissolved the committee or continued to raise questions and objections about the ministry. But his sense of call and his response to the children's needs were strong enough to draw him into a deeper commitment. It seems the Spirit wouldn't let him off the hook.

When God called Ronald to this ministry, Ronald faced quite a bit of risk. The first risk came when he acknowledged to himself and his pastor that he felt the need of the at-risk children had to be addressed. Serving as chair of the committee when he was unsure about his role and his commitment was also a risk. Yet it seems to me that he took the greatest risk on the day that he stood before his fellow officers and confessed that he felt the call of God to this ministry. Once he acknowledged the call, he was bound more tightly to it, and the risk of failure hung heavier over him. Fear of failure and the possibility of being exposed as a failure made the decision difficult.

The factors that I've highlighted in Ronald's case figure prominently in every call, whether to ordained ministry or to a special ministry in the church or community. Getting the call in motion always involves choice, commitment, and risk. There's no way around it: answering a call always involves risk.

The call of God to ministry exists first in the mind of God as a potentiality. It remains a mere possibility until the person and the situation coalesce through the power of a call. God waits for the right moment and for the right person.

The call finds receptivity in the heart and soul of that right person. God's call awakens a new possibility in his or her heart. The possibility of this call not only meets a human need but also fulfills the person who humbly responds to it.

Active response to the call incarnates the will of God in human history. The potentiality of the call unites with the possibility of human action to result in the creation of a new situation in history.

God is glorified through the actualization of his will in people who obey his call. Human beings are fulfilled by responding to the possibility created by the action of the Spirit of God upon them. Human history becomes infused with the holy through the obedience of God's people. This new history created through the Spirit is lifted into the life of God and shares in the eternity of the Father, the Son, and the Holy Spirit.

I know that these theological assertions sound abstract to clergy and laypersons alike. Perhaps some people find these bare statements without much meaning or persuasive power. But I think it will make a difference if we look at Ronald's experience though these lenses. I'm particularly concerned that we realize that the faithful actions of human beings in response to God's call have eternal significance. What greater motivation could we receive than the opportunity to participate in the eternity of God through our obedience to his call?

Long before Ronald recognized his call, that call resided in the mind of God. From the foundation of the world God knew Ronald, loved him, and purposed good for him. Perhaps God even destined him to be a man of compassion and humble service. Yet this intention of God awaited the proper moment. The convergence of Ronald's restless spirit and the pain of abused children provided the context in which the Spirit uttered God's call. Ronald heard that call and, although he struggled with it, found a way to respond to it. The God revealed in Jesus Christ is not the passionless god of Greek philosophy but a God of love and compassion who rejoices when his creatures honor and obey him. God was pleased with Ronald and the members of the body of Christ who heard the call through him.

When Ronald returned from Vietnam and eventually settled in his hometown, he wasn't consciously seeking God's will for his life. He was attending church, worshipping God, and seeking to live a godly life, but he didn't exhibit a deep intimacy with God. However, his service in Vietnam, the disappointment and pain he experienced in California, and his search for the right job combined to give him a feeling of unsettledness. Without always being aware of it, Ronald was driven by his restlessness and lack of direction. Something inside of him knew that he was made for more than working, making a living, and dying.

When he agreed to teach a parental course in communication, he was unaware that he had stepped onto a pathway that would lead him toward the fulfillment of his life. At the time he accepted the challenge, it seemed the natural choice to make. His efforts to help parents of abused children rewarded him with a new kind of peace and fulfillment. Still, he didn't realize that he was on a course that had a profound God-dimension to it. Only after his visit to the three schools and his conversations with the principals did he begin to wonder if God was guiding his steps.

When his minister and his church's governing body responded positively to his proposal to help the at-risk children, Ronald felt more confident that God was "messing with his life." But this confidence was challenged by his reluctance to give himself completely to the call. Months of conversation and struggle finally brought him to the retreat and the presentation of the challenge to the leaders. The whole process of discussing the mission and his finally embracing the leadership was a period of increasing commitment to God's call.

The change in his appearance between the first day I met him and the last time I saw him told its own story of joy and fulfillment. Here was a man who had been led by God and sent to a mission that had fulfilled his life more than human affirmation or material acquisition ever could.

When I review this personal call and the resulting choices that occurred, I see an act that is not only transcendent and incarnational but also eternal. The call that Ronald experienced originated in God. It was God who took the initiative to call him gently and gradually into a ministry to abused children. Those visits to the schools, the cards and letters sent to the students, the hours of tutoring, and the times of mentoring shared by Ronald and the members of his congregation made visible and tangible God's intention. God was at work in their work. God was present not only in the pain of the children but also in the expression of grace and love. Through this ministry, the grace and love of God were mingled with the lives of faithful followers of Christ and the pain-filled lives of abused children. God was honored. God was glorified.

But I believe that more than incarnation was taking place. This ministry of compassion now resides in the all-knowing mind of God. Because it is in God's memory, it will last for ever and ever. God is glorified not only in small acts of compassion but also in the memory of these events. When I consider what our loving obedience means to God, it lifts my sense of fulfillment to the highest level, because I know that what is done in the name of Christ lasts forever.

To be a servant of God is therefore no small thing, because we participate in the continuing incarnation and ascension. Buried in obedience, raised in life-giving fulfillment, and ascended to the Eternal. Isn't this what it means to do the will of God?

Exercises in Discernment

1. Live with your sense of call for several weeks. If you have peace and clarity about the direction of your call, take further steps to obey it.
2. If you feel called to a ministry in your local church or community, consider taking the following actions:
   - Invite several people to form a support group who will pray with you about the ministry.
   - After praying for a clear vision of your call, make a list of first steps to be taken to implement it.
   - Get approval from the minister and/or governing body of your church, and proceed with the vision.
   - Create a timeline showing when each step will be completed.
   - Plan to make regular reports to the governing body about your ministry.
   - Keep looking to God for guidance.
3. If you feel a call to ordained ministry, the following steps of obedience will assist you in your call:
   - Select a small group of friends who will pray for you and support you in your response to God's call. Meet with them and share your plans.
   - After talking with your minister and your church's governing

body, contact several seminaries of your denomination. Request catalogs and ask to be placed on their mailing lists. They will gladly comply.

- Read the catalogs and course listings to see which schools seem right for you.
- Ask the admissions director of each school for a schedule of weekend conferences to which prospective students are invited. Make plans to attend one of these conferences at two or three of the seminaries.
- Choose a seminary and proceed in faith that God will provide.

4. Whatever your call, make a list of the help you will need to be faithful to God and God's call to you.

CHAPTER EIGHT

Living into the Call

Embracing a call from God must move us steadily toward being fully embraced by the call of God. We don't possess the call; the call possesses us. We can't live into the call in a detached way, as if we sat at a giant computer manipulating the keys. Rather, being embraced by the call is much more like being washed over by ocean waves and drawn out into the depths. As we begin living the call, it increasingly becomes incarnate in our thinking and our actions; the call becomes flesh in and through us. It isn't like a rock tossed into a pail that simply falls to the bottom with a thud. The call is more like a sponge that drops into a bucketful of water and soaks itself full. Or like a teaspoon of blue dye dripped into a glass, coloring all the water in it.

Reggie: A Concrete Example

I know a man on the West Coast who better illustrates what it means to live into a call than anyone else I've ever met. In my first conversation with Reginald, whom I soon learned to call "Reggie," he told me about a profound mystical experience that had been a major turning point in his life. He had been running up a mountain trail behind his house when he paused to catch his breath. And then it happened. Suddenly, without any warning, and with no intentional searching on his part, he had a profound sense of being engulfed by the presence of God. He knows that this experience wasn't simply a "runner's high" because he had experienced that before, and this revelation was different. He struggled to describe it to me. God was there; he experienced a profound sense of joy; he felt the moment had meaning for his future but had no clue about what that would be.

At the time this event occurred, Reggie wasn't a Christian, but he did believe in God. In fact, he had believed in God since his sophomore year in college, when he had had a similar experience. He had been studying the arguments for the existence of God. Then, without any effort on his part, and quite without warning, he heard a voice speaking softly inside him, assuring him of God's existence. The voice was something like what Saint Paul described when he spoke of a yearning "too deep for words." From that time on, Reggie never doubted the existence of God.

But let's get back to the encounter on the mountain, which was the kind of experience that illuminates other experiences. Reggie said that at that moment he had a sense of mission, perhaps a calling, but at the time he was too wrapped up in his family and his business to pay attention to it. But this brush with the transcendent left him with an appetite for the Spirit; he wanted more. He had always been fascinated with the historical Jesus, so he took Jesus as his initial starting point. While searching the Internet for more information, he came across this statement: "If you truly want to know what it's like to experience Jesus Christ, read about the experiences of the early Christians in the Book of Acts." So he began reading the stories in the Acts of the Apostles and comparing their experiences to his own. They were similar, and he felt less strange.

He began to expand his reading about and exploration of the early Christians, and this broader search brought him into contact with several mystical writers. While reading the writings of one of the mystics, he realized that their language described his experience exactly: it was his native land; he had come home. Theological dogma had never spoken to him; it seemed so abstract and removed from life. But the writings of the mystics were grounded in their experience of God. He found that their testimony enlightened his encounter with Jesus of Nazareth.

I asked him how this experience of the living Christ was related to his sense of call. After a few minutes of thoughtful reflection, he said, "God is inviting us into a relationship with Jesus Christ." For him as a Christian, everything was rooted in Jesus. And because of this relationship with Jesus, he experienced the presence of God and lived with a great deal of joy; he had a hope of eternal life and took delight in being part of the continuing incarnation of Jesus in the world. Reggie also confessed that the relationship between God and the living Christ was still a mystery to him, as it is to most of us.

The call he received charged him to help other people hear the invitation of God. Hearing God's vague invitation on the mountain, and later the more specific invitation through Jesus Christ, shaped his idea of helping others hear the invitation. He felt compelled to reach out to skeptical people like himself for whom traditional language produced only indifference. He focused his attention on the experience of God and on helping others enter into it. He couldn't imagine anything of greater worth or deeper fulfillment than helping others turn to God and listen to God for themselves. He was convinced that hearing God would change the orientation of their lives completely, that they would be transformed from self-centered people into kingdom people. Confining his language to God made it easier for him, and confessing his own struggle with how God and Christ are related seemed to offer a bridge to others who were also struggling with this faith issue.

As this call deepened, Reggie decided that he had better find a place to nurture it. Rather quickly he came to the conclusion that locating a church would be his first step. After visiting numerous congregations, he found one that seemed to honor the experience of God that was changing his life. He began attending there. He also enrolled in classes at a local seminary to learn more about this God who had invited him into this marvelous relationship. After months of searching for a way to help people hear the invitation of God, Reggie came up with the idea of starting a group for skeptics: an anything-goes, no-question-is-too-dumb, begin-your-quest-where-you-are group.

At the time Reggie and I spoke, the skeptics group was about a year old. Reggie was still searching for more effective ways to invite people into the conversations. Each week he made slight changes in the way he conducted the group — an action/reflection model of learning through hands-on experience. After being involved with the group for a year, he was now thinking about how to standardize the program and "package" it for other churches. How could he distribute it? How could he train leaders? Already he was beginning to think about research into language that communicated with outsiders to the faith.

Sensing his profound passion for helping others hear God's invitation, I began to wonder how this avocation affected his vocation. When I inquired how his faith related to his work, he had a ready answer. First, he admitted that his passion for the ministry side of his life competed with his business. His energy was in evangelism, but business was a necessity. His response didn't surprise me. He lamented the fact that he didn't know how to bring his sense of God more deeply into his business and also into his family life. (I realized later that he probably wanted to talk about family life, but I didn't pick up on it at the time.)

Being interested in the fusion of faith and work myself, I asked him what issues he faced in bringing his two worlds together. After a period of serious reflection, he said that he listened to people in his ministry in a different way than he listened to customers and suppliers at work. It wasn't that one group was important and another wasn't, but rather that issues of faith piqued his interest and his energy more than business matters. Just the admission of this difficulty caused him to restate his desire to fuse his faith with his business.

Perhaps this notion of God in the everyday seems as common as Kleenex, but it isn't known and practiced by all the baptized. In fact, a friend of mine was sharing her experience of seeking constantly to be before God every day of the week, and a fellow listener said, "I've never thought of Christianity like that before." How do you suppose she had been thinking about it?

I continued trying to understand Reggie's experience of God. "Where do you get the energy for this work?" I asked. "Where do you get the energy to keep your ministry alive and to be creative in it?"

"I pray a lot," he answered.

"But isn't there anything else that gives you the energy you need to keep at the task?"

"If there is, I can't think of it."

I began to reflect on his experience with him. "I suppose that you've been launched into this ministry with so much spirit and enthusiasm that during this brief period you haven't had time to burn out. Aren't you finding a source of strength in the spiritual direction group you belong to?"

"Yes, I am," he said, "and I also talk often with my minister. She seems to understand my sense of call and the passion I have for the work." He paused briefly, then continued, "I've participated in several silent retreats sponsored by our church, and recently we had a discernment retreat that meant a great deal to me. Maybe I've been finding more nurture than I've been aware of. I suppose I've been nurtured in ways that I didn't notice or name at the time."

As we talked, I had the distinct impression that this man was being dealt with by God as clearly and powerfully as anyone that I had ever known. The clarity of God's presence in his experience prompted my next question: "Did you ever think that God might be calling you into ordained ministry?"

"Yes, I have — I've thought a lot about that question. My clearest sense of call is to spread the message so that others may hear the invitation of God. When I thought about ordained ministry earlier, I felt considerable resistance to the idea, but I don't feel so strongly about it now. But I'm fifty-one years old, and in some ways my age works against my move toward ordination."

My exploration of his call took another turn at this point. "Did you ever think about starting a church?"

"Yes, often. I think that would be challenging, and some days I feel that I'd like to try it. But to start a church would mean being ordained first, and I haven't felt a strong enough leading toward ordination to form a congregation."

"What's your vision for the future?" I asked.

"I'd like to evolve the skeptics ministry into a clearly defined approach to outsiders to the faith. Once I've been able to do that, I'd like to develop materials for other congregations to help them begin their own groups for skeptics. I think there are six or seven additional ministries that could flow from my work with skeptics. Emphases on prayer, the Bible, and Christian witness come immediately to mind."

As I listened to this energized man talk about his vision for the future, I suggested that he might like to accelerate his seminary training, because a degree would legitimate him as well as inform him. I wondered aloud if he might become an evangelist under the authority of his church's governing board. As an evangelist he could work in congregations, lead retreats, and speak at worship services with legitimacy.

This is an amazing story of awakening and call that clearly shows many aspects of a serious disciple living into the call of God. I'm amazed at the manner in which the Lord encountered Reggie. His attending to this encounter through reflection, prayer, information-gathering, enrolling in seminary, and beginning a seekers group are all matters of wonderment to me.

Ways to Live into Your Call

How does a disciple appropriate the call he or she has received? The story of Reggie's experience illustrates one answer to this important question. Using this interview as a backdrop, I want to offer four specific suggestions for living into your call.

Live in Awareness Daily

To live in awareness means to notice what's going on in your life and in the world around you. It means being in tune with yourself as well as being sensitive to what other people say both with words and with body language. The antithesis of living in awareness is sleeping your way through life, living unconsciously, automatically, and thoughtlessly. People who live like this appear to be "pre-recorded," on automatic pi-

lot. How many people fit this description! Living this way is a temptation for all of us, but to yield to it dulls our sense of call and blunts our ef-
fectiveness.

In a lay vocation, this temptation lures people into set ways of thinking about how work is done, how relationships are established, and how
goals are pursued. Life becomes predictable, with little variation from
one day to the next. Living this kind of routinized life works in opposi-
tion to living into the call.

For the pastor, the temptation to serve people out of a sense of duty
or out of habit leads to coldness and insensitivity to the pain of those
people. It makes preaching a recital instead of a proclamation, and it
turns administration from discernment into management. At this stage,
the once-exuberant minister begins to lose passion and vision. Before
too long, the memory of why he or she went into ordained ministry
fades.

Surprisingly, the student in the seminary faces similar temptations.
The pressure to study tends to eliminate extended times of prayer and
silence. As a consequence, the sense of call that brought this serious disciple to seminary grows dull, and the focus on being chosen for ministry
gets blurred by the urgency to get a job. When the sense of call moves to
the margin of consciousness, the passion for ministry cools, and the
would-be apostle becomes a professional.

What dire consequences for failing to pay attention! Is there no an-
tidote to this sleepwalking?

Indeed there is. Wake up! Slap yourself, pinch yourself, or stick
yourself with a pin, figuratively speaking. Stop. Look. Listen.

Here are a few hints that may help. First of all, stop the unconscious
procession of your life by paying attention to what's happening right before your eyes. Really look at the earth and sky and trees. Notice the
people around you; look at their faces. Listen when people speak to you.
Examine the thoughts that flow through your mind. Do these things,
and do them *now*. Without correction, your little canoe of consciousness may be floating nearer to treacherous falls. Start paying attention
to where you are every moment. Come to the present.

You can reclaim your awareness if you intentionally shut down your automatic responses to life for a few moments every day. Create small spaces during the day in which you intentionally think about your life before God. Consistently pausing several times during the day will help you to turn off the automated functions of life and put them under manual control.

Whenever you take these pauses — at the beginning of the day, or during busy hours on the job, or at the end of the day — you might want to employ a few small exercises that will help you. First, discover the art of wondering. In moments when you've stopped the unconscious process of your life, wonder about what's going on in your life. Where is God in your life today? Why have you met and spoken to someone you didn't expect to meet? Why are you running so fast? These little springboards of wonder can help you feel the depth of life beneath the agitation on the surface. You'll find wonder very friendly to your commitment to live intentionally.

Another helpful daily exercise calls for using your imagination. Imagination, the capacity to envision life as it might be, can become a powerful ally in overcoming spiritual somnambulism. One day when I was taking a walk with my neighbor and friend Walter Brueggemann, he told me a story that has stayed with me. He had been reading an account of a Jewish man who lived far from his homeland and felt the daily pressure of a social world unsympathetic to his faith and values. When asked how he survived in such adverse circumstances, he answered, "Every day I rise from sleep and imagine myself a Jew." Each day presented him with the challenge of re-envisioning himself as a Jew. Without this daily practice, the cultural pressure would likely have squeezed this awareness of his Jewishness right out of him.

What I'm suggesting through this story is that every day we must imagine ourselves as Christians, as people called by God in Jesus Christ and as people who live in unity with our Lord. We must imagine a world in which life and vitality shimmer beneath the surface of every event of our lives. And we must imagine ourselves living with openness to the presence of God in all things. When we've fully developed this practice, our ways of automated living will have been seriously challenged, if not left behind for good.

Reggie illustrates one way of becoming aware. When he was running up the mountain and was encountered by the Spirit, he paused and listened to what was said to him. With his appetite for the Spirit whetted, he began a search for words and symbols to grasp and develop his faith. His efforts to bring his new sense of God into his work life further illustrate the way in which an aware person functions. Before that day when he was jogging the mountain trail, Reggie thought of himself as spiritual in a general sort of way, but his awareness of God came in brief periods separated by months — even years. From the time of his awakening, all experiences pointed toward his growing awareness that God is a part of everything. While Reggie was making these discoveries, another friend of mine — Richard — was doing the same.

Early on I introduced you to Richard, a young attorney who was seeking to discern whether he had a call to ordained ministry. After I suggested that he return to his hometown and live for God there, he did. When he got home, he invited his minister to join with him in forming a small group of men who met weekly for prayer. Through the inspiration of the Spirit received in that group, Richard began visiting every minister in town, asking them about their Christian faith and learning from them. In a sense, he became the ecumenical bond pulling together all the different faiths in the area. With the blessing of his pastor, he began teaching a class focused on the Holy Spirit each Wednesday night at his local church. Attendance grew rapidly. Next, the governing body gave him permission to invite a local Pentecostal minister to speak to the growing assembly on Wednesday nights. Richard's emphasis on the Spirit and how to discern the Presence in everyday life eventually led to a ministry to the poor of the community that involved providing food, clothing, counseling, and legal representation. The day he was approached about becoming a judge, he felt the hand of God was redirecting his life. Richard's life had been taken off automatic pilot, and the Spirit had been given manual control.

Be Creative in Your Ministry

A ministry has never been born fully grown. A vital ministry is always growing and expanding into new areas. When you're called to a ministry, begin small, begin with certain specific expectations, and begin immediately. Think of the ministry as a tiny plant that has broken the ground's surface with a tender shoot. This emerging plant requires attention, nurture, and cultivation. With this kind of care, the plant will grow and continue to change.

Each achievement in a ministry manifests a type of growth, and this growth provides grist for the imagination mill. When a group of women perform their music at a nursing home and interact with the residents, their reflection on this experience will yield new ways of performing their service. Each time a mentor visits with a student in a special school, she will get new ideas about how to be with the child in more helpful ways. In Richard's case, every minister that he visited in his hometown gave him new insight into the religious life of the community and suggested ways that his Christian work might improve. To help keep your ministry alive, review each act of ministry as a way of listening for God through the work of your hands.

A few suggestions may help to you to keep your creativity fresh and productive. First, look at the basic data of your present ministry — who, what, how, and why. How can it be improved? How can it be expanded? Every ministry can be done better and more effectively.

Second, be willing to take risks. Risk underlies developing a ministry as surely as it does beginning one. Change always involves risk — the risk of loss, the risk of failure, and the risk of giving up control. The risk of beginning a ministry lies in the the possibility of failing to get it off the ground, but once it's functional, change creates the risk of altering or destroying the ministry. The larger a ministry becomes and the more people it involves, the more resistant it will become to change. What most people don't realize is the simple fact that refusing to change will kill a ministry as surely as making wrong or ill-timed choices.

Third, give wings to your imagination. God has given us imagination as an instrument to create the future. Those who study learning in children say that a child will be stuck in a preliminary developmental stage until he or she learns to think by analogy: "This is like. . . ." When a child defines one thing by comparing it with another, he or she is taking an analogical leap. For example, when my grandson says, "This dog is like a horse because he has four legs," he's using his imagination. We can use our imagination in the same way. If I, for example, teach a course as an instructor, I can imagine myself teaching as a facilitator. Envisioning the difference in teaching requires the creative use of imagination.

With respect to ministry, when you understand one way of performing the ministry, you can imagine doing it in a different way. The imagination can act upon the "difference" and anticipate the outcome of the changes. The imagination offers a great deal of help in acquiring knowledge, creating "newness," and anticipating the results of change. No other experience can equal the sheer delight of using the imagination. But before releasing your imagination, be prepared to take risks. Imagining a new thing come very close to participating in God's creativity.

Fourth, mentor new leaders and workers in the ministry. A ministry could hardly be called creative if it didn't develop the next generation of leaders. All the people who are participating in a ministry will be trained to do a particular task, but successfully performing a task is quite different from being a leader. A man in my church leads a Habitat team, but if this ministry is to continue effectively, he must mentor some of the team members so that they will be able to assume leadership roles. This principle applies to all ministries.

Fifth, be willing to let a ministry die. I can think of nothing sadder than seeing a ministry continue when the need for it no longer exists. This perversion occurs when maintaining the ministry becomes the goal rather than meeting the need for which it was begun. There is extreme resistance to stopping a ministry when endowment has been created and salaried persons depend upon their association with the ministry for their livelihood. Nevertheless, a ministry's viability must always be the most important factor. Ministries arise because of a current need, and when that need no longer exists, the ministry should be allowed to die.

Once again, I believe that we see in Reggie's ministry a number of the initiatives that keep a ministry alive. Because he had been a skeptic for so many years, it was quite natural for him to create a ministry for skeptics. He wrote material for the group to study that I helped him revise. After conducting his first group, he evaluated the results and determined to find better ways to promote the group in order to attract those who would benefit most from it. He saw deficiencies in the material and revised it for the next group. After a year of working with his original concept, he began thinking about how to get the ministry into other churches. Because of his success with the early groups, Reggie imagined spin-offs that responded to other questions from inquiring members. When I mentioned the Internet as a natural channel for expansion, he had already thought of that — he was already far ahead of me in his dreams. Do you see how a dynamic leader is always thinking creatively about ways to improve and expand a ministry?

Find Ways to Keep the Call Fresh

The passage of time need not erode your enthusiasm and dreams for your ministry. You can take initiatives to keep your call fresh. "Fresh" doesn't mean "the same." I think that many of us feel a constant urge to revisit our original call with the hope that the emotions accompanying our acceptance of the call will return. Such efforts to manipulate our feelings are generally unproductive. While we can't dictate our feelings, we can take several steps to keep our sense of call focused and fresh.

Talk about Your Sense of God in Your Ministry   Many in my tradition feel ill at ease when speaking about God. That's due in part to the culture of the church, and in part to a lack of clear conviction about the presence and activity of God. Frequently when the call of God goes unidentified, the focus shifts from the providence of God to the tasks of ministry, and this shift leads to doing a job instead of following a call.

Ministers particularly fall into extended sessions of shoptalk about their congregations, discussing the number of members, the number of regular attendees, building campaigns, and the size of the budget. If the conversation veers from these old standbys, it may center on the hottest social issue and what the liberals or conservatives are saying about it. Such conversation does little to enhance a minister's sense of call.

Over the past four or five years, a friend of mine who's a minister has been experiencing a spiritual transformation. He was raised in a Presbyterian home, educated in the classical Reformed tradition, and has been an effective minister for more than a quarter of a century. Several years ago he began to experience significant changes in his life. In addition to facing a serious medical problem, he faced changes in the church he pastored. His training hadn't prepared him for lay men and women experiencing a call, and he had never before seen such profound changes occur in the lives of ordinary people. These changes paralleled changes that God was effecting in his life. He shocked me one day when he said, "Since God has begun working in my life in such a dramatic fashion, I'm bored with the conversation of my liberal friends. When we get together, issues and opinions dominate the discussion, and God is seldom mentioned."

I freely acknowledge that there are those extremely pious people, always talking about God with every breath, who can be equally boring, and I don't encourage that kind of God-talk. But my friend's comment makes a good point: we need to learn how to talk with others about the work to which God has called us. We should acknowledge both the presence and the absence of God in our pursuit of faithfulness. And we should speak in a way that suggests that we know it is God's ministry and we participate with God in getting it done.

What about you? Are you openly talking about God in your ministry?

Keep Your Life Balanced   Imagine the difficulty of developing the skill needed to walk a high wire. Some famous high-wire artists have developed the skill so well that they walk at great heights under difficult conditions without so much as a safety net beneath them. This feat is not only dangerous but also difficult to achieve. This image hints at the difficulty most of us experience when we try to strike a balance in our lives between family, social life, church, work, and call.

I once spoke with a young doctor, probably about forty years old. He made it clear to me how deeply he felt about his practice and his desire to help people with their health issues. God seemed to be at the center of his work and the fulfillment that he experienced. At the same time, he was lamenting the fact that he worked a sixty-hour week, saw too little of his children, had no time for social engagements, and lacked quality time with his wife.

When a person with great gifts for ministry feels utterly fulfilled by what she or he does, balance appears to be an unreachable goal. But without that balance, he or she will be exposed to the fierce fire of burnout, which will be inevitable. Balance almost certainly keeps the call fresher and makes the individual less prone to burnout.

I felt a sense of balance in the woman I met who was called to minister to sexually abused children. When I asked her to tell me what was happening in her life, she spoke of her interest in reading the Bible and studying through the Bethel Bible Series. Her eyes lit up when she talked about sitting by the pool and talking with her husband about God. I knew that she was getting control of her life when she indicated that she and her husband had begun to tithe. I was further convinced that she was gaining balance when she listed her priorities as God, family, and work. I wouldn't expect early burnout for her.

Take a close look at your life. Does it have the kind of balance that you need to sustain you?

Accept Appreciation and Affirmation　Being capable of receiving appreciation and affirmation also helps keep the call fresh. This isn't as easy as it may sound. Did you ever notice how difficult it is to affirm some people? They seem to have a shield up to block out affirmation and gratitude. When you begin to affirm them, they become embarrassed and deflect your well-intentioned affirmation of their skill or helpfulness. When you express gratitude, they likely discount your appreciation by claiming that what they did was nothing. Every one of us desires both affirmation and appreciation. Why do some of us find it so difficult to accept them?

This isn't the place to explore the psychological aspects of self-worth, or the early teaching of well-meaning parents, or the fear of responsibility that might motivate those individuals who resist our offerings. But it is the place to acknowledge that God has made us to love and be loved, to appreciate and to be appreciated. When we reject love and affirmation, our lives are impoverished.

When people express love and appreciation for you, it will help you to hear them if you realize that they're reporting their feelings. They aren't primarily giving you information about yourself; they're telling you how they experience you. Can you receive what they say and rejoice with them in their experience of God in you? By God's grace, you are worthy of affirmation and gratitude. Receive them with gratitude to God!

Be a Lifelong Learner and Teacher   Finally, be a lifelong learner and a lifelong teacher. In a sense these two go hand in hand — learning and teaching. If a person continues to learn, it is natural for him or her to share that learning. There are numerous ways to keep a fresh sense of calling through learning. Attend continuing education classes, surf the Internet, read books, talk with informed people, and reflect on your experience. In today's world there's no shortage of information on any subject that engages you. Your ministry can stay fresh if you feed new information into your experience.

And be generous with what you learn. You'll realize that your own sense of calling stays fresh when you mentor others and pass on to them what you've learned about the ministry in which you're engaged. Passing on insights and skills to others will rejuvenate your own spirit and enrich your ministry.

Even when we've done all these things to keep our call clear and strong, we still come to places in our lives that demand a deeper refreshing, something that we cannot orchestrate, something only God can do in us. This need drives us to re-dig the old wells of call and drink from them.

Uncover the Wells of Renewal

The ancient text of Genesis gave me this metaphor of the wells from which we draw fresh, living water:

> Isaac planted crops in that land and the same year reaped a hundredfold, because the LORD blessed him. The man became rich, and his wealth continued to grow until he became very wealthy. He had so many flocks and herds and servants that the Philistines envied him. So all the wells that his father's servants had dug in the time of his father Abraham, the Philistines stopped up, filling them with earth.
>
> Then Abimelech said to Isaac, "Move away from us; you have become too powerful for us."
>
> So Isaac moved away from there and encamped in the Valley of Gerar and settled there. Isaac reopened the wells that had been dug in the time of his father Abraham, which the Philistines had stopped up after Abraham died, and he gave them the same names his father had given them.
>
> Isaac's servants dug in the valley and discovered a well of fresh water there. (Gen. 26:11-19, NIV)

This brief narrative unmasks our ancient enemies of jealousy, fear, and greed. Isaac had been too successful in breeding livestock and multiplying his wealth. He had become a threat to the Philistines, and thus King Abimelech asked him to move out of Gerar. There was no place for him to go but the desert, where he needed water more than anything else. To obtain it, Isaac reopened the wells that had been dug by his father, Abraham. In a single simple sentence the writer gives us a picture of what happened next: "Isaac's servants dug in the valley and discovered a well of fresh water there" (Gen. 26:19). The original wells had been dug a long time before, but they had been filled up and covered over by the Philistines. But Isaac's servants found those old wells, cleared out the debris, and discovered fresh water still flowing to those wells.

As we make the journey with Christ, living out our call, we learn practices and disciplines that open up the wells of the Spirit within us. And then we become distracted and forget the things that we learned. Our lives dry out and become barren. We are driven from the safety of old abodes and thrust into a land where it is hot and arid. Our thirst for water grows, and when it becomes great enough, we dig out the old wells.

My friend Reggie hasn't yet come to this point, but he will one day. We all do. When I spoke with him, he was so filled with the rapture of his vision and the new insights he had gained that the thought of dryness wasn't even crossing his mind. But the day will come when the circumstances of his life hurl him up against the solid walls of Abimelech, and he will be stunned and driven into the desert. In the desert he will feel such an unquenchable thirst that he will look for the old wells and dig them out again.

My friend Anthony, whom I wrote about in an earlier chapter, reached this point a while ago. He called me one day out of the blue and said, "I need to talk with you."

When I recognized his voice, a picture of him flashed into my mind: a man in midlife who had left all the security he had ever known to come to seminary to prepare for the ministry of Christ. He had felt called. He had come with great expectancy that God would use his life. He had taken a number of my classes.

Anthony ended my little reverie with a muffled cry for help. He began by reviewing the last several years. He had served a church successfully. The church members were friends; some had even become good friends. They paid him a decent salary. He had the freedom to do things in the larger church and serve as a counselor and guide to others. His life seemed so good in many ways — but in other ways it was collapsing.

This short review of his life led to a painful confession. "Something crucial is missing in my life. I preach from my head most of the time, and when I'm preparing the sermon, I often wonder if I believe what I'm planning to preach." With painful pauses he moaned aloud, "How can I preach something that I'm not connected with? I feel so phony."

These opening confessions seemed to break down the dam, and

there flooded from his lips months of pent-up pain and fear. "I'm plagued with doubts about God. I'm even questioning some orthodox things that I've believed all my life. My doubts and my loose-jointed faith are affecting other parts of my life too. Some days I feel like I'm falling apart."

I was listening to a devout and serious soul who had been thrown against the walls of Abimelech and had been cast out into the desert of testing. I sensed that he was holding things together — but just barely. What do you say to a man who's in the midst of a life-and-death struggle?

I knew that I couldn't pronounce a cure over the phone. But when a soul is desperate, you have to make an effort. I suggested that he try to get his bearings by answering the question "What's going on in my life?" You can't begin looking for a well until you have your bearings.

I followed this recommendation with the suggestion that he dig up the "fresh water" of companions. This is important for all of us who find ourselves in a hard place: to seek out those who can understand what we're facing and talk earnestly with them. God speaks to us through brothers and sisters.

Fearing that I would burden Anthony with too many tasks, I refrained from suggesting that he find a place of silence so that he could be still before God. People wandering around in desert experiences may need to scream out their pain, and spewing it out is good. Screaming gives us enough relief so that we can come to a quiet place and get silent enough on the inside to hear.

I never talk with a friend who's standing in the desert without asking if I may pray for him or her. When I asked Anthony if I could pray for him, he agreed. After saying a few words, I paused before the "Amen." When I finished, Anthony said, "I wish you could see the tears streaming down my face. It feels so good to weep. Now I know why your name came to me while I was walking last night."

I paused to give thanks for Anthony and his witness to me. Like many followers of Christ, I too struggle with receiving affirmation.

When individuals like Anthony or you or me come to desert places, we're often tempted to believe that God is displeased or angry with us. I don't rule out the judgment of God, but that explanation offers only one option. Maybe God is using this period of dryness and testing to signal to Anthony that this phase of his ministry is coming to a close. Or perhaps this time comes to prepare him for an important mission that God has for him. From the beginning God has used spells of dryness to awaken his people from the paralysis of their automated living. These alternate interpretations hopefully will lead us — Anthony, you, and me — into a consideration of life between various forms of God's call.

Exercises in Discernment

This chapter has addressed the challenge of keeping the call alive. The suggestions apply to those who have newly embraced a call to pastoral ministry, to those who have received a call for ministry in the church or the community, and to pastors who have been in the field for a number of years. All those who are called by God need refreshment.

1. Write a summary of your life experience for the past week, noting the following: when were you aware of God during the week, and how, in retrospect, you can see how God was at work in your life during this time. Write a prayer that expresses your gratitude to God and your desire to be more open to God's presence.
2. Describe one way that you can be more creative in your present ministry. (For seminarians, "present ministry" means being good students.)
3. Complete each of the following sentences. Write short paragraphs of explanation.
   - I would like to tell a friend that my call. . . .
   - My life would have more balance if. . . .
   - I find it difficult to receive affirmation because. . . .
   - My work would improve if I gave more attention to studying. . . .
4. Recall times when you have felt refreshed by the Spirit. Describe one of these in your journal. What can you learn from this experience that would be of help to you now?

CHAPTER NINE

From Call to Call

The call of God has many faces, and yet there is but one call. What may appear to be multiple calls in a person's life hide the fact that God's one call is a summons into a relationship with Godself. This one, original call takes many forms. For the ordained minister of God, the call may have begun with a call to seminary, followed by a call to a church or some other form of ordained ministry. For the layperson, the single call begins with his or her baptism into the community of faith but may also manifest itself subsequently in several vocational changes. This call into a developing relationship with God also manifests itself in different ministries within the church — teaching a class, serving as an elder, working with youth. Or the call may be similar to the various ministries that we've identified throughout this book. All these different forms of a call from God flow from the one call.

Change is inherent in our vocation, whether it is in the church or in the world. The pattern of change takes the shape of a transition from one form of the call to another. For example, a woman may feel a call to seminary, and after a period of discernment she enrolls in a seminary and studies for three years. In her last year of seminary training, she begins seeking another form of the call: pastor of a congregation. She is installed in a church and guides it for five or six years. When she grows restless, she senses that her call to that particular church is ending. She begins seeking another call or resigns from her current position to await God's guidance. When the new call comes, she responds and begins to weave her life and energy around the new call. This brief example illustrates what I mean by the phrase "from call to call." The dynamics of this experience seem to be attachment, detachment, transition, and reattachment.

Two Stories of Transition

Sometimes theological descriptions of the call become so abstract that they're either boring or obscure. To avoid both of these problems, I want to work with concrete stories of women's and men's experiences, focusing on two stories in particular.

A Layman's Vocational Story

I've known Timothy for nearly a quarter of a century. To me he is the embodiment of faithfulness and self-giving. His story shows the nature of a single call taking several significant forms over a lifetime.

Timothy can't recall a time when he wasn't involved in the church. His parents, who were of modest means, took him to Sunday school and worship, and these early experiences shaped him in the faith. The stability of his family shifted when his father became ill and died. Because of his father's early death and the family's lack of financial resources, Timothy never expected to get a college degree. But, by the providence of God, unexpected doors opened for him, and after attending two different institutions, he received his degree.

During his college years, Timothy — unlike many students his age — maintained a relationship with God and the church. At times he considered entering the ordained ministry, but after a hard-fought battle with himself, he decided that he wasn't being called to ordination. Following college, he enlisted in the Marine Corps, got married, and set out on his journey. After serving as a Marine for four years, he listened for the call of God that would use his gifts in the fullest possible way.

His first place of service was with the Boy Scouts of America. As an executive he was responsible for raising funds, conducting camps, and enlisting volunteers. He threw himself into the work as if the fate of the organization rested upon his shoulders. Such bold, sacrificial service got the attention of his superiors, and they advanced him to greater roles of leadership. This meant spending many hours at work, away from his family, and moving frequently around the country. This took a heavy toll on his wife and daughters.

Timothy expected to spend his working life with the Scouts and maybe one day head the organization. But this dream was not to be, despite his dedication and hard work. Because of a false report in his file, due to a few misrepresentations of the truth shared in the leadership ranks, and the politics of the organization, Timothy hit a dead end.

Facing his situation head on and evaluating it honestly forced him to see that his future with the Boy Scouts was over. When he described this situation to me, he said, "When this happened, I felt angry and disgusted with the leadership that had undermined my calling. I had always thought that if I was committed, worked hard, and kept my relations clear, I would succeed. When things didn't turn out that way, I was depressed, frustrated, and critical. I began looking for another call."

In a matter of weeks he became the development officer for a local university. The transition to the university was simple for Timothy, and he enjoyed the sense of fulfillment he got from creating a better world through funding educational endeavors.

His relationships at the university stood in sharp contrast with those in his previous job. The academic dean, who was his immediate supervisor, appreciated him deeply, and invited him to the table with the other deans. Timothy successfully raised money for new chairs in the business school and other departments.

Timothy spent ten years at the university, which brought him a sense of personal fulfillment as well as rich rewards financially, socially, and spiritually. He expected to remain at the university until retirement. But then came a new university president who had his own plan for development and someone he wanted to implement it. Very quickly Timothy saw the handwriting on the wall and began seeking guidance for his next call.

That next call wasn't long in coming: Timothy was offered the position of development officer at a Catholic hospital. Perhaps he got this call because of his excellent work at the university, or perhaps in part because of the book he had published on aspects of fund-raising. Whatever the case, his sterling faith and his life of dedication fit well with the faith and work of the Catholic sisters at the hospital. Through his efforts, funding for the hospital increased 15 percent a year for the first six or seven years. He was amply rewarded professionally, financially, and emotionally.

After Timothy had served the hospital for ten years, the scene began to change. Health-care organizations, including hospitals, were having a difficult time breaking even financially. The hospital leadership lacked a clear vision, and the support Timothy needed for major projects simply wasn't forthcoming. Again he began to feel increasingly frustrated. At this point he was in his early sixties, and he began to think about retirement.

Perhaps he could find two or three good clients and work for them at a slower pace. Then he could spend more time with his wife and daughters and grandchildren, hopefully making up for being away from home so often when his family was young. These possibilities appealed to him, and he set a date for his retirement. All in all, his experience at the hospital had been one of the best of his entire working career.

When he was sixty-four, Timothy retired. His hopes to work freelance for a few clients didn't work out. Various alliances didn't produce new income, and he had to face the fact that maybe his paid working years had come to an end. But I don't think this conclusion bothered him particularly. From day to day he waited to see where the hand of God was leading him — to doing more work in the church, volunteering in the community, and spending more time with his family. After a year Timothy concluded that perhaps he was being called to be a good grandfather and a volunteer who would help churches and nonprofit corporations develop funding efforts.

This experience of call illustrates how being called into a relationship with God may find expression in several different contexts. It also reveals the soul of a man who has been faithful to God in each of the contexts in which he's served. Furthermore, Timothy's story reveals a way to deal with calls that are interrupted by events beyond one's control. Although Timothy has always felt God's hand in his life, reviewing his vocational history reinforced his faith in the providence of God. Similar discoveries can be made by those individuals who find themselves in transition between calls.

A Pastor's Transition

I first met Bernard when he enrolled in a Master of Theology program at Columbia Theological Seminary. At the time, I was teaching spiritual formation and Christian spirituality, and he enrolled in several of my classes. His experience in the church illustrates quite clearly the phases of the call that I outlined earlier: attachment, detachment, transition, and reattachment.

Bernard spent the first nine years of his ministry in a small church in a small town in North Carolina. The church's story is not unlike that of many other congregations, and Bernard's experience there was predictable. After he finished his seminary training, this congregation called him as their pastor. The church was located in a cotton-mill village that had been built and paid for by the mill owner. When Bernard first got there, the congregation was made up of a a fairly homogeneous group of people.

Most seminarians begin their ministry with vision and vitality, and Bernard was no exception. He began visiting church members and then the residents of the community, seeking to strengthen the church and broaden its outreach. But things changed when the mill closed shortly after Bernard arrived. When that happened, the people who lived in the area and attended the church got better jobs elsewhere and moved away, but they still drove back to their old community for Sunday worship. Meanwhile, as the original residents moved out of the area, others moved in. When new people from the community came to church, they weren't warmly welcomed by the original members, perhaps because most of these new people were from a lower socio-economic group.

Bernard made sincere efforts at outreach, but when church members reacted negatively, he backed away from these "outsiders" too. He worked hard, kept his anger suppressed — and became exhausted. All this time he was betraying his deepest convictions.

After seven years of frustration, he began looking for help with renewing the church's life and his own life as well. He attended a conference called "How to Have a Grace-filled Church." The title of the conference attracted him, and the thought of it inspired him. At the conference he learned many things that could help renew and redirect the congregation. But the most important thing he learned was that a grace-filled church must have a grace-filled pastor.

Full of inspiration from the conference, this searching pastor returned to his little church and began preaching grace. Perhaps he was adapting to his situation John Wesley's direction to Methodist preachers: "Preach on faith until you've got it, and then preach it because you've got it." Whatever the case, Bernard preached on grace. The people who had recently moved into the community heard him gladly, but the old members of the church rejected the word of grace as too permissive. They demanded rules, standards, and performance because they were still living under the law.

Bernard kept preaching grace and reading the fathers of the church — Irenaeus, Augustine, and Chrysostom. His preaching and his including the poor from the neighborhood soon precipitated a crisis in his church. The tension finally became so great that he decided to leave. He announced his plans six months before his departure. During the time between his announcement and his actual leaving, he was able to reconcile with the people, help them buy a piece of property in the suburbs for a new church building, and keep his integrity in the process.

When he and I sat down to talk, he told me about the pathway to Columbia: "It took me a year to detach myself from that congregation. I had served them for nine years, and I knew it was time for me to leave. During that time I'd gotten all the life sucked out of me, and I had to get close to God again. I felt called away from that situation as surely as I had felt called to it." His sense of detachment had grown as strong as his earlier sense of attachment.

During the transitional year he spent at Columbia studying for a Master of Theology degree, he didn't stop ministering. He found a ministry to international students who were lonely and in need of friendship. Many of them needed transportation too, and Bernard felt called to help them get around the city. He ministered to these people in their loneliness and confusion, and they loved him for it.

Although he was involved in this ministry, Bernard focused mainly on his spiritual quest. He read spiritual classics, attended classes, wrote papers, and met with a small group for fellowship. He experienced the luxury of spending time in study and prayer, and he narrowed the distance between himself and God. Both his life and his vision for ministry changed. And his marital status changed too: he fell in love with a woman who was attending Emory University, and they were married.

I asked him how he sustained himself for a year without a salary. He explained that he borrowed $20,000 to live on while he studied. When he told me that, my respect for him and his response to God's call escalated.

I asked Bernard if he had felt anxious about not having another call as the year drew to a close. He told me that that period had certainly been a challenging time for him. He had to write a thesis, but he also had to tend to his ailing parents, which meant moving into their home for a while. He missed the Columbia community, and found it difficult to work on his thesis in the isolation of his parents' home. But he wasn't anxious about his call.

"How did you get to your present place of ministry?" I asked.

The question sparked both fire and delight in him, and he continued his story: "I made myself available, and a certain church received my personal information form from the denomination. This church had recently been through a disillusioning experience with a minister who had accepted their call but then backed out at the last minute. This disappointment drove the whole church to gather for prayer and discernment concerning their calling the next pastor. When they contacted me, I felt that they had wrapped the call in prayer. When I accepted the call, the presbytery had reservations about placing a minister who believed in spirituality in an urban area, but they finally approved my call anyway."

My inquiry about how his work was going drew a lively response. "I've never been so fulfilled in my life," he told me. "This small church is filled with gifted people who feel God's call to minister to others. One of the members with a call to preach couldn't leave his job to attend seminary. So I sent him to a nursing home and told him to create a congregation there. Now he preaches to them every week.

"Another talented elder wanted to work with the thirty-something group. He's currently gathering people in the suburbs for prayer and Bible study. We plan to begin a church there in a few months.

"We've also opened our building for other groups to use. We have a Hispanic congregation meeting in our building, and also a black Pentecostal congregation. Something is happening in our building every day of the week."

"What accounts for the amazing success you're having?" I inquired.

"We changed the paradigm from church to kingdom," he explained. "We're concerned not with building a church but with being kingdom builders — and we're doing that. Not only did we change the paradigm; we got structures out of the way and connected passion with purpose.

"In my presbytery they've now dubbed me 'the guru of redevelopment.'" This powerful sense of reattachment has confirmed Bernard's personal and professional renewal.

Detaching from a Call

Almost all of the people I've consulted about life between calls have mentioned the sense of detachment they've felt. And restlessness almost always accompanies the waning of a call to a particular ministry.

Jacob had been minister of First Church for ten years when I talked with him about the awakened individuals in his congregation. While discussing his relationship with them, he told me that he was planning to resign from the church in six weeks. Why did he think this was the time to leave?

"I'm beginning to feel restless and less enthusiastic about ministry in this particular call," Jacob explained. "I'm not burned out — I know what that feels like. But I am experiencing an inner detachment from this church and from these people."

Not in response to any particular question from me, Jacob began ruminating aloud. "I don't think I'm running away from anything. I don't feel any particular distaste for the people or the situation. I simply think I've done all that I can do for these people, and now they need different leadership. I have no idea what will happen to me when I don't have the responsibility of preaching every week. I can't imagine myself not being a pastor. The prospect of the future is frightening — but also exciting."

I've always admired Jacob's honesty and integrity. As I listened to him, I knew that I was hearing a man speak with unblemished honesty about critical matters of his life and his soul.

Jacob's sense that his call was ending was prompted by his growing internal restlessness; for my lay friend Timothy, on the other hand, the signs of the end were external — and very sudden. After having dedicated fifteen years of his life to the Boy Scouts organization, he ran into a brick wall. He had no chance to assume a position of major leadership, and I think he accurately read that closed door as a signal to leave. The door had closed because of the misjudgment of others, and Timothy was understandably frustrated and angry. But I do believe that God speaks to us in our anger and frustration just as he speaks to us in our delight and fulfillment. And in Timothy's case, God was using that moment of rejection to prepare a special place for him, one that would bring affirmation and fulfillment far beyond what he had experienced in the Scouting organization.

Bernard's disengagement from his congregation came about because his visions and hopes for the church conflicted with theirs. His efforts to enlarge their vision failed; his decision to accommodate their desires led to burnout for him. Over a period of several years, his energy dried up, he lost enthusiasm, and then he began to doubt himself and his call. The conference that he attended on becoming a grace-filled church gave birth to a new vision in him. This fresh glimpse of life gave him enough courage to risk resigning from the church and also the faith to borrow money for living expenses for a year while he went back to seminary.

Detachment always occurs either through loss of interest or the birth of a new and more challenging vision. Sometimes these two signs converge. If you're in a ministry that drains all the energy out of you and you can't find ways to renew yourself, pay attention to your loss. If you lack a sense of fulfillment in your ministry and you don't feel your work has worth, start to suspect that you're detaching yourself from a call — or that you're being detached from a call. Also, when you feel something inside you pushing you away from a particular ministry, listen to this inner voice. When you begin to think about doing something else, following a different pathway or beginning a new ministry, take heed. God may be working through these shifting interests and emotions.

The experiences of Jacob, Timothy, and Bernard all seemed to be the prelude to the ending of a call or to their personal detachment from a call. The feelings they experienced can also signal burnout, a state of listlessness and emotional paralysis. If you're suffering from burnout, there are ways to respond other than leaving. You can consider reorganizing your schedule to get either more rest or greater distance from your work — or both. And making certain that your tasks match your gifts will open ways for you to deal with this barren condition. Burnout can also be healed with retreat and the renewal of mind and heart.

The symptoms that plagued Jacob, Timothy, and Bernard may also sometimes indicate a deeper call into ministry. This deeper call may have aspects of doubt and barrenness that testing burns away. The pain of the desert or the darkness has a way of purging the soul of dross.

How does one distinguish what the symptoms mean? This can be a challenging matter. Even serious disciples may need help in discerning whether their inner state indicates burnout or purgation.

Ending a Ministry

The symptoms we've just discussed may signal the need for renewal or be an invitation to greater depth. But they can also signal the end of a ministry, as they did in the cases I've described. Ending a ministry shouldn't be looked upon as the result of failure or incompetence or lack of dedication. There often comes a time when one should end a ministry or end one's connection with a particular ministry. In fact, one of the great tragedies in a life's work is to perpetuate a ministry when its day has passed.

In 1963 I conducted the first Lay Witness Mission. During the next decade this ministry grew — from a single mission to a thousand being conducted in a single year. More than 50,000 laypersons had become involved in this weekend renewal event. They came from congregations across the nation. As the ministry grew, we passed on the concept to a dozen other denominations, which soon developed their own programs.

Thirty years later I was invited to speak to a gathering of people who were celebrating the anniversary of the mission's birth. As I looked around the room, I saw the faces of men and women who had been with me when I began the ministry. The work had been good and fulfilling for them and for me, but these people were still holding on to a dream whose time had passed. I had moved on, but they had not, and I grieved for them.

How do we know when a ministry has ended? How do we know that a particular ministry should be ended? There are telltale signs that exist in every ministry, from congregational programs to specialized ministries in the church and in the larger community. I'll use my experience with the lay mission to illustrate these signs.

First, a ministry should cease when the need that prompted it no longer exists. The lay mission I started spoke to the need for renewal, and that need didn't go away — but most of the churches that intended to host lay missions had done so in the first decade after the program was started. Repeating the mission in a particular congregation only led to a stylized experience for a clique in the congregation. I suspect it also gave birth to some unhealthy expressions of the faith.

Second, a ministry should cease when those who began it sense that its original purpose has been fulfilled. No ministry should be perpetuated for its own sake. The original dream of the lay mission I started was to bring renewal to laity in congregations. It did bring renewal — but it didn't grow to include the new needs that stemmed from its success.

Third, a ministry should end when new people don't feel a call to engage in the task. In the early days of the lay mission program, there were more people who felt called to serve as leaders and witnesses than we could properly equip and train. By the end of the second decade, however, most of the workers were the ones who had begun with me. This wasn't a good sign.

Fourth, a ministry should end — or be passed on — when God gives us a vision for the next stage of the ministry. Even as I write this principle, I realize that the original dream may feed the new vision, and if it does, the original vision should be passed on to other individuals. Visionaries must go beyond the original dream or die. Freeze a prophet's vision, and you kill the prophet. It is his or her destiny to see a vision and pursue it, and then to see a new vision.

Several dire consequences follow when a ministry whose day has passed — or nearly passed — continues. When you examine a ministry that has effectively died but is still perpetuated, you notice that the people engaged in it continue old patterns as if nothing has changed. This, of course, is like selling iceboxes in the age of refrigerators.

Those who perpetuate a dead ministry idealize the past and live on the memories of earlier exploits and accomplishments. When the ministry treasures its stories of yesterday's successes, a tradition develops into an impenetrable shield, and it protects the participants from the cold winds of reality. When the tradition has been in place long enough, it takes on a sacred character, and ceasing or changing the ministry is viewed as dishonoring God.

Perhaps the most tragic consequence of perpetuating a ministry that has died is the widening of the distance between the workers and the ministry, and between the ministry and God. A ministry that once was vibrant and alive with the Spirit has died, but the devotees of the ministry refuse to bury the corpse. This is a difficult but necessary task. As the ancient tribal wisdom of the Dakota Indians has it, "When the horse is dead, dismount!"

When a ministry has died, the creation of a new vision and the recovery of hope might make a difference, but generally there is no thought of either one. When people are trudging through the present while focused on the past, the future doesn't exist. What could be sadder?

Living through the Transition

One of the most difficult disciplines in the period of transition is wait-ing for the new door to open. Jacob feels fear mixed with anticipation while he waits for a new direction in his life. Timothy struggles with what to focus on after his retirement. Moving from a day filled with ap-pointments to a day that might be punctuated only by a phone call from a friend strips things down to basics. Perhaps Jacob and Timothy — and you — would be helped by the experience of Parker Palmer. I know his story — which he relates in *Let Your Life Speak*[1] — was illuminating for me.

Parker finished his Ph.D. at Berkeley and went to Washington, D.C., as a teacher and community organizer. I think he believed this was the right move to make. But after five years in that ministry he was burned out, and he didn't know the way forward. Since he was a Quaker, he knew about the Pendle Hill community, a Quaker center for study and contemplation in Wallingford, Pennsylvania, near Philadelphia. He asked to stay there for a few months so that he could get his bearings and find a way into the future. Because this was a community of faith and prayer where there were mature people of discernment, he felt certain he could get help in resolving the issue of his call.

Soon after he arrived, community members admonished him by saying, "Have faith and way will open." They spoke of "way," not "the way" or "a way" but the unmodified "way." When I first read this admo-nition in the book, I thought the definite or indefinite article had been mistakenly omitted. As I continued to read Parker's story, however, I soon discovered that if this was a mistake, the storyteller made it consis-tently. He constantly spoke about "way" opening.

But "way" didn't open for Parker. He became discouraged, thinking that maybe something was wrong with him. One day he went to an elder in the community and confessed to her, "I sit in the silence; I pray; I lis-ten for my calling. But way is not opening."

This wise and mature woman told him that she had been a Quaker

1. Palmer, *Let Your Life Speak* (San Francisco: Jossey-Bass, 2000), p. 38.

from birth — for more than sixty years — and way had never opened in front of her. Of all the words that Parker could have heard, these seemed like the worst. If "way" had never opened for her, how could he expect it to open for him?

While he was in the midst of his anxious thoughts, she added, "But a lot of way has closed behind me, and that's had the same guiding effect." This was indeed a wise observation. Looking back at what has closed may indicate that we have taken the right pathway. So in our waiting for "way" to open before us, we might do well to see how "way" is closing behind us. A greater certitude of direction may come in retrospect than in prospect.

Because of how old I am today, there's a great deal more retrospect than prospect in my life. Over the course of a lifetime I've been through numerous transitions. What I've said about endings and beginnings has been greatly influenced by my own experience of passing that way. Writing about how I experienced "way" twenty or thirty years ago comes rather easily for me, but I find it more difficult to write about "way" in the present transition that I now face.

For more than fifty years I've been a serious Christian, and during those years I've been a preacher, a minister of a church, a director of a parachurch organization, and a professor. In all these roles I've been what I would call a religious entrepreneur. The drive to create, to seek the new way of being a minister or doing ministry, has characterized my life. In June of 2000 I retired as the Professor of Christian Spirituality at Columbia Theological Seminary.

Retirement represents the ending of a ministry in a way I haven't experienced before. Before I retired, there were signs that were pointing me in that direction. I felt that my work as a professor had ended. I had done what I could do for the renewal of clergy by challenging aims and modes of current theological curricula. I had been fulfilled in that calling, but I knew it was drawing to a close. In the last year of my ministry, my wife, who also worked as my secretary, noted that it was winding down.

What is my life like in retirement? My body has spoken to me from time to time, but shortly after retirement it shouted at me. All in all, though, my health is good. Through the years my wife and I have been able to save a little, generous people have helped us along, and a monthly check from the government now provides adequately for our basic needs. So the issue of my life is centered on one question: What does God want me to do with my life now?

I don't believe that retirement signals the end of ministry. I'm called to minister until I die. What form should it take in this new situation? When I first retired, I planned to take the first year off, but I think I got cold feet. So instead of doing that, I booked it full with retreats and month-long stints in three churches. All this changed when I experienced what my friends at the wellness center call an "incident." I took the "incident" as a gentle rebuke to my strong-headedness. Still, I face the question of what God intends for me now.

I don't feel discouraged, nor do I feel depressed. I'm not shocked by this turn of events. I'm fully aware that God's timing seldom matches my desires, but I know that God's time is the right time.

A few days ago while I was taking a walk, words came into my mind that sounded like Godspeech: "You have been in this place of not knowing before, and I have shown you the way in due course. Can't you trust me now to reveal my will to you for these remaining years of your life?"

With that word, I wait in confidence that "way" will open before me — or close behind me.

Exercises in Discernment

In this chapter I've shared my insights into detaching yourself from one call in order to seek a new call. If you're a seminary student, this may mean delaying training until you have greater certainty about a call. If you're a layperson in a ministry, detachment may mean that you've finished a certain task God had for you to do. If you're an ordained minister, you may need to consider leaving one call for another.

As you consider the ending of one ministry and the beginning of another, honestly answering the following questions will help you. Think deeply about each of these questions and write the answers from your heart.

1. Am I still fulfilled in this ministry? Does it still meet the needs for which it was begun? Or is this ministry really finished?
2. Is my "wilderness" a call to something new, or is it a call into a deeper relationship with God? (Record the evidence for each of these possibilities.)
3. Can I let go of my security and my present identity to embrace the new thing that God has in mind for me?
4. Do I trust God for the next call? What are my fears and hesitations at this juncture?

CHAPTER TEN

Dealing with the Living Stones

W hat a strange and wonderful thing is occurring as we begin the twenty-first century! God seems to be renewing the Church of Jesus Christ in a new and powerful way. The renewal originates not in human strategy and technological innovations but in God's Spirit working in the lives of the people. There are no rules of engagement incumbent upon God, and so God, with perfect freedom, initiates calls in a broad variety of ways. The dozen or so stories in this book about men and women called by God reflect this diversity. For those of us who are watching for the call of God to evidence itself in others, this diversity prompts us to look more closely for the divine fingerprints.

If this dramatic encroachment of the Spirit is God's way of awakening and calling lay men and women into specific ministries, we must become more astute in our listening for God. This task weighs heavily upon us because last century's ministers lacked training in the discernment of the Spirit, and the present generation of theological students isn't much better equipped. As a consequence of this impoverishment in both training and experience, many clergypersons are frightened by these rather novel acts of God. Their fear often leads them to ignore, suppress, or forthrightly oppose what seems to them pure fanaticism. I don't dismiss their fears lightly. I too am afraid of genuine fanatics because they can do irreparable damage. But for the most part those individuals being called by God are not fanatical. Most need sympathetic, spiritually attuned pastors who can assist them in discerning God's intention for their lives and clarifying how this intention relates to the congregation.

I raise this point because it is a crucial matter when the Spirit acts among us. Pastors need perspective, spiritual sensitivity, and skill to engage these God-called individuals face-to-face, enter into their discernment, and serve as their spiritual companions. Members of the congregation need clear guidance in discerning God's call in others because this task rests heavily upon them as well. Lay men and women who have been awakened by the Spirit also need guidance for living in the community of the baptized. Many of us can relate examples of individuals who seemed rather extreme in their behavior after a special movement of the Spirit in their lives. But I recall an old saying credited to Methodist bishop Arthur J. Moore: "It's easier to tame a fanatic than it is to raise a corpse."

In this chapter I refer to those who have had a spiritual resurrection as the "living stones." It's a phrase drawn from Scripture: "As you come to him, the living Stone — rejected by men but chosen by God and precious to him — you also, like living stones, are being built into a spiritual house to be a holy priesthood, offering spiritual sacrifices acceptable to God through Jesus Christ" (1 Peter 2:4-5, NIV). "Living stones" is the name Peter gives to new people coming into a relationship with Christ. They are made alive through his church and are joined together with the mortar of the Spirit to form a Temple of God, a holy dwelling.

The phrase "living stones" resides in my deep memory. It goes back to my college days, when I memorized the Letters of Peter. Recently I've made several trips with pilgrims to Israel, and we've gone to Ibillin to see Father Elias Chacour, a Palestinian (Melkite) priest working for justice. When we visit with him, he always says to the pilgrims, "Don't spend all your time looking at the dead stones that cover the ground. Get to know the living stones." He is eager for pilgrims to engage Palestinian Christians in conversation about the land and about their Lord.

Woven into every chapter of this book are stories of individuals who are no longer dead stones detached from the Temple of God; they've become vital, living stones. Here's one more story.

Six or seven years ago I was invited to help a congregation plan and conduct a weekend evangelism conference. The conference focused on the evangelistic task of the church: to reach outside the walls to invite and include others in the family of God. During the course of the event, I met a few individuals who cared deeply about this phase of the church's mission; they wanted their church to grow. The chairman of the event had many gifts and was deeply committed to Christ's ministry through his congregation. All of us worked hard, but very little came out of the weekend. It was a big push, but in the end we didn't have much to show for our efforts.

Recently the minister of that same congregation invited me to conduct an officers' retreat there. When I met these leaders again, they were a totally different group. Something dramatic had happened since I led the conference on evangelism several years earlier. These officers had come alive spiritually. Their eyes gleamed with a new joy and an assurance of faith. They had an openness to God that I hadn't seen during my earlier visit. They spoke eagerly about their faith and exhibited a deepened hunger for God. A number of them spoke freely about God's call to them and their desire to discern God's will clearly and follow it. This group of Christians reminded me of the New Testament church described in the book of Acts. The Spirit among them was alive, exhilarating, and magnetic. I wanted to be part of the transformation that God was working in their community of faith. The question of what to do with these "living stones" arose naturally out of my interaction with them. How did the pastor, who had been raised in a traditional congregation and trained in a classical Reformed theological seminary, respond to this work of the Spirit? Doubtless he led with fear and trepidation. On the one hand, he didn't want to squelch the work of the Spirit. But on the other hand, he didn't want a group of zealots to alienate lifelong members of the church. Other pastoral and lay leaders shared his concern and worked to preserve the unity of the church.

This community of "living stones" raises many broader questions about leadership and relationships. Pastors of congregations with renewed people like these need to rethink their leadership style and retool themselves for a different kind of ministry. When individuals in the faith community experience the presence of God in fresh and some-times miraculous ways, it creates dis-ease in pastors with fragile faith and also in pastors with great needs for control. The pastor in this situa-tion had made some painful yet positive changes. Through the working of the Spirit, he had revised his vision for ministry, his style of leader-ship, and his way of preaching.

Carol's Story: A "Living Stone" Speaks

In the first chapter of this book, I described Carol as one of those indi-viduals who was being awakened to the Presence and as someone who was pursuing a ministry of loving care to those in her church. To initiate a concrete way of thinking about how "living stones" help to renew con-gregations, I want to tell you about further developments in Carol's life.

After our initial conversation, she entered our Certificate in Spiri-tual Formation program at Columbia Theological Seminary, and I had occasion to visit with her periodically over the next three years. During one of our last visits, she told me about a gift that had begun to manifest itself in her life — the gift of healing.

The awareness of her gift came to her in a strange way. One night she was awakened from sleep by a strange burning in her heart. It seemed that her heart was being opened wide and love was pouring in and out of it. With the heat came a profound sense of the presence of God. She was overwhelmed by the encounter. After that, when she met people in pain, she was almost overcome by their suffering. The warmth and sense of love flowing from her lasted for three or four months. Dur-ing this time she began to recognize that the love in her heart was flow-ing to others in the form of healing. When she told me that, I asked her to give me some specific examples.

She told me how a Jewish man, a friend of her and her husband, had been diagnosed with two brain tumors presumed to be malignant. He was understandably frightened, and because he knew of Carol's gifts, he asked her for help. She explained to him that she was a Christian and that her ministry was through Christ. She asked him if that would be a problem for him. "No, Carol," he said. "I trust you in whatever you need to do."

Before he arrived at her home, she prepared herself with prayer. She had candles burning and soft music playing to aid her in continued prayer. After her friend arrived, she began by asking God's help in the healing. The peaceful atmosphere, with Christian music playing in the background, helped her remain in a spirit of prayer. As her friend became quiet, she began moving her hands through the space above and around his body, "smoothing out" the energy fields and acknowledging her desire for him to be healed and made whole. As she was praying, she suddenly and unexpectedly felt her hand being drawn toward his head. Her hand became intensely hot, and when she looked at it, there was a ray of light the size of a half-dollar beaming from her hand into his head above the temples. The ray appeared about the size of a pinhead where it entered his body.

The man for whom she was praying was an engineer who was trapped in the world of Enlightenment. When she finished praying, he said to her, "I felt everything that you did. I guess I'm going to have to rethink many things about my perspective." While the power and the light seem quite miraculous, Carol said the greatest miracle that day was the peace that her friend felt. "For the first time since I heard about the tumors, I'm at peace," he told her. "I've been so frightened and disturbed that there's been nothing but fear and confusion in my mind. Peace has completely escaped me." When the surgeons operated on him the following week, they found a mass of tangled blood vessels — but no tumors.

This man was only one of many people Carol was praying for. People had begun coming to her, desiring her prayers for physical healing, deep emotional healing, and the healing of relationships. Her pastor frequently sent people to see her. She always offered herself fully and freely to be an instrument of God.

Still, this gift came with a price. With honesty and frankness, Carol confessed to me the struggle she had been having with this new ministry. She had liked her life as it was. The heavy demands for healing began to change her life, and she didn't want it to change — and neither did her family. Her husband was very important to her, and she treasured their relationship, but he was getting edgy about her spirituality. Her children were asking if she was "getting weird on them." So strained family relations added to the burden of offering prayerful healing to so many people. As a result, she became more resistant to her gift, often wishing she didn't possess it.

She went away on retreat, seeking a resolution to her inward struggle. As she wrestled with herself, she came to the conclusion that she didn't want the gift because of what it was costing her in so many areas of her life. At one point she boldly told God, "I'm not accepting this gift of healing." As she spent more time in quiet reflection, however, it became clear to her that rejecting the gift was also rejecting the Giver of the gift.

When she left the monastery where she had been on retreat, she was still struggling. Shortly afterward a woman whom she had seen at her church but didn't know personally rang her doorbell. Carol asked her in, and the woman asked if Carol could pray and read a few verses of Scripture. After Carol did so, the woman gave her a disturbing message. She began by saying that there had been several times in her life when she had met someone and God had spoken to her at the moment of meeting. She went on to say that when she met Carol, she experienced that phenomenon of the Spirit. Then she said bluntly, "You've been chosen to receive a gift, and you haven't been very receptive to it or grateful for it." Standing in Carol's kitchen that morning, the woman addressed all of Carol's fears and affirmed that God would use her. She promised Carol that God would also provide for her, take care of her, and protect her. After she prayed for Carol, she left.

Afterward, Carol felt angry and stunned, as if she'd had her hands slapped. "What's happening?" she asked herself. "I'm just trying to maintain a degree of normalcy in my life, and along comes this gift that threatens to disrupt everything." Still, in spite of her fears and her reluctance, Carol made a vow that day: "I won't say 'no' to God, and I'll trust God to take care of me and my family."

This account isn't the end of Carol's story. It may not even be the midpoint. Somehow I knew that day when she first sat in my office that

God had destined her for something special in his mission to the world. She is indeed one of God's "living stones."

Jacob's Story: Illuminating the Pastoral Role

How does a pastor who's been trained in a classical theological tradition respond to those individuals who have been awakened by the Spirit and have been given gifts and callings for ministry? I think the people whose stories I've told in this exploration of call have, without exception, gotten good responses from the pastors of their churches. Perhaps that's one reason why all of them have been able to begin and carry on effective ministries. But their experience could have been very different.

For example, I spoke with Jacob, a pastor of the old school, who was very honest with me about how he had responded to "living stones" earlier in his ministry. He told me that when he was pastor of a church that had individuals "like those" in it, he preached three or four sermons aimed directly at them. "That's about all it took," he explained. "In four or five weeks most of them had left to go to other churches. I made a point of meeting with those who didn't leave and suggesting that they would probably be happier in another church. Those were the days when I preached and lived completely in my head, and I had absolutely no sense of the presence of God in my life." His aim was to lead a strong traditional congregation in worshipping God and in making the community a better place to live. How could this man effectively guide people who were being called by God for mission?

I asked this pastor what had changed his perspective from one of antagonism and rejection to one of encouragement and support. He gave me a thoughtful and truthful answer: "When the pulpit committee from my current congregation met with me while I was considering their call, they said, 'We want a pastor to lead us in evangelism and spiritual nurture.' I didn't know exactly what those terms meant to them, but to me they were quite vague. When I accepted the call, I committed myself to listen to those types of people that I had always written off before. I soon discovered that this congregation had a number of members who spoke freely about God and their experience of God. They expressed their desire to be closer to God and to know God better. I resolved to listen to them and try to understand what they meant. The depth of their hunger and the persistence of their searching began to wear off on me. So I became a seeker for something more in my life and ministry."

He continued with this frank confession: "I still haven't lost all my anxiety about those people who have deeply religious experiences, but I've seen enough to know that there is a reality beyond the realm of sight and touch. I've become convinced in both my mind and my heart that there's a different level of faith that I'm beginning to experience. I wouldn't call myself a teacher of this way, but I am a serious student."

Not all pastors have the kind of resistance to "living stones" that my friend Jacob had at the beginning of his ministry. But, unfortunately, many still do. In the coming church the need for the spiritually sensitive pastor will increase as the Spirit continues to call. What specific roles does the awakened, spiritually sensitive pastor need to play in the lives of "called" individuals?

1. The pastor needs to be an encourager of the people. When any of us begins the way of obedience, we feel fragile, and our first steps are tentative. We need affirmation and encouragement to persist in the way.

Not long ago I spoke with a woman friend of mine who pastors a church in New Jersey. Since her arrival at that church, the attendance has gone through the roof. More importantly, she and the congregation share the conviction that God is at work in their midst. I asked her what she did to nurture the life of faith in God's people. She said simply, "I love them and encourage them in their ministries."

When I asked my own pastor what he thought "awakened" individuals needed most, he didn't hesitate to say, "Encouragement!" He expanded on this response by saying that the pastor's bias should always be toward saying "yes," affirming those people and supporting their call from God. To make his position clearer, he contrasted the encouraging pastor with the typical mainline minister, who is often analytical, critical, and skeptical. Too many pastors serve as gatekeepers, and many seem to have a bias toward keeping the gate shut.

2. The pastor needs to make space for everyone in the congregation.

How many people in a congregation feel marginalized? How many feel that their ideas and opinions don't matter? How many awakened members also camp on the margins? Without the pastor's help, the people whom the Spirit is calling forth will feel ostracized and marginalized. Through preaching, teaching, and personal contact, the effective pastor assists these people by helping them find their places in the life of the congregation. This new day in the church calls for practices that contrast sharply with many commonplace practices in last century's church.

When I asked my friend Jacob how he responded to the vital people in his present congregation, he searched his memory. "When this congregation called me here to focus on evangelism and spiritual nurture," he recalled, "I knew that we would need a large umbrella under which to gather the great diversity of people in the membership. So I saw my role as opening the largest umbrella I could find." Making room for the newly awakened — what a delightful task!

3. The pastor needs to be a theological resource for the congregation, especially for those whom God is calling for lay or ordained ministry. Some congregations differentiate between the experience of the Spirit and the knowledge of Scripture and theology. This is a false dichotomy. Growing disciples need to know the teaching of Scripture and the thinking of the historical church; this will aid in their spiritual formation. If we don't reflect on spiritual experience, it is vulnerable to perversion and often turns into fanaticism. Good pastors help members of the body of Christ understand and assimilate their experiences of God.

4. The pastor needs to be a good listener. In fact, listening may be the most important gift that a pastor can offer an awakened individual. When a person hears himself or herself talk about the work of God in the soul, it not only helps him or her sort out a call but also provides sought-after and much-needed acceptance. Without a good listener, such self-expression is impossible.

Not only does a person sort out experiences while expressing them, but he or she also gives a discerning pastor important personal information. The Spirit uses this information to help the pastor discern the work of God in that person's life. And when the pastor has these conversations with a number of "living stones," he or she develops a multifaceted picture of the Spirit's work in the community of faith.

Listening to someone may be the greatest affirmation that we can offer him or her. What greater honor can you bestow upon a person than the dignity implied in listening? This gracious act unmistakably demonstrates your interest in that person and communicates a feeling of importance.

Perhaps the reason that some pastors can't listen is that no one ever listened to them. It's particularly difficult to listen to another when you yourself feel unheard. A pastor's need to speak can plug up a perfectly good pair of ears. Those pastors who feel that they have no one to listen to their struggles perhaps need to listen to themselves, to determine what their inner self is trying to say so that they can break through the barrier that keeps them from listening to others.

5. The pastor needs to serve as a spiritual guide. In this book I've recommended that those who have new experiences of God consult with their pastor. When they do so, they will inevitably have questions about what's happening to them. In these instances the pastor assumes the role of spiritual director. He or she doesn't supply answers to the searching church members, but instead listens and seeks to discern with them where God is at work in their lives.

While these aren't the only roles that pastors fill in their congregations, the roles I've identified are crucial and offer important starting points. Each of these roles helps nurture the new life of the Spirit so that it matures in the awakened individuals and has a leavening effect in the larger church. If genuine change is to occur, it must include not only the "newly activated" members but also the longtime traditional members. I hope that pastors will protect the new life being born in their congregations, care for those who find themselves attached to the old ways, and ultimately lead the church in change as it responds to the Spirit.

In light of the ultimate vision for the new church, I will now speak to the "living stones" about a few things they need to acknowledge and practice.

A Word to the "Living Stones"

When issues arise in the congregation because of the awakening of some members to the Spirit's presence, not all the problems arise from the longtime traditional members. People just coming into the stream of the Spirit often contribute to the tension and confusion themselves. In light of this situation, I want to make a few suggestions to those people who have had a fresh encounter with God and are filled with enthusiasm.

1. Remain humble about your ecstatic experience of God's presence. Don't get the notion that you are now superior to your fellow Christians and that they are second-class Christians until they have an experience similar to yours.

I think you would do well to emulate Carol's example. In her pain she was warmly embraced by divine love. The healing presence of God came without being invited and surrounded her with kindness and mercy. Her life was changed, and her spirit was healed. She spoke with her pastor, but she didn't "advertise" her experience of God to others. When people began to notice the change in her, they sought her out.

Even when the fire of God burned its way into her heart, she didn't go out and tell others about this holy encounter. In fact, the gift of healing that came along with the fire of divine love made her feel embarrassed rather than proud. Here's a person who first met God in an amazing way and was given a significant ministry through God's Spirit, but she didn't take herself too seriously. I've never met a person who showed more humility and exemplified greater dependence upon God than Carol.

Ecstasy in the Spirit has a way of turning off common sense, but Carol's example shows that it needn't be that way.

2. Resist the temptation to privatize your faith. Christ has called you to express the body of Christ, not to be a solo performer. The ministry doesn't belong to you; it is Christ's. Recognize that you are one member of his body and that you need the support and encouragement of fellow Christians, just as they need support and encouragement from you.

Perhaps of all those whose stories of call we've explored, Ronald demonstrated sensitivity to the community of faith most clearly. When he began to feel a call to minister to the children in special schools, he went immediately to his pastor and talked with him about the challenge. Later he took the need to help these children to the governing body of his church and invited them to participate in meeting that need. Many of them heard the challenge and responded to it.

As a result of Ronald's looking to his church community for assistance and support, thirty or forty people had the privilege of participating in the ministry to which he felt called. Because he based his ministry in the church, it had not only legitimacy but also accountability.

Those of us who privatize our ministry deny the church the privilege of working with us, and we lose both the protection and the challenge that the church offers.

3. You are a contemporary witness to the living presence of Christ — but don't forget that a trail of witnesses two thousand miles long stretches out behind you. The present generation has a tendency to ignore history and fall into the illusion that they must be discovering everything for the first time. I believe this to be especially characteristic of people who are awakened by powerful ecstatic experiences. Both Carol and Reginald have had such experiences, but unlike many, they have looked to the tradition for guidance.

Since both had such powerful, life-changing encounters with Christ, they could easily have turned inward for assurance and wisdom without consulting the long tradition. Fortunately, neither of them took that route. Reginald enrolled in a seminary to study the documents of the faith and the interpretations of it by God's people through the ages. Carol enrolled in a program in spiritual formation to increase both her knowledge of Scripture and her knowledge of the Christian tradition.

One person's lifetime is too short to use as a yardstick for the measurement of truth. No issue confronts us today that hasn't in some form challenged Christians in another era. People with as much dedication as we have today have sought the wisdom of God in living out their lives in obedience. Many of these faithful disciples have left us records of their successes and failures. We are foolish if we don't familiarize ourselves with this ancient wisdom.

If you want to know about the faith of God's people, read the Bible. If you have an issue of discernment, review the sayings of the desert fathers and mothers. If you're seeking balance in your life, read the rules of Saint Benedict. If you have a problem with pride, consult Francis of Assisi. The faithful — like Saint Ignatius, John Calvin, Martin Luther, John Wesley, Jonathan Edwards, Thomas Merton, and Henri Nouwen — offer the followers of Christ much wisdom on scores of issues. Remember that you stand on the shoulders of all those who have preceded you, and that you have much to learn from them.

4. Continue to grow as long as you live. There is no limit to spiritual growth. Drink more and more deeply of that hidden river of reality which flows beneath the surface of life and participates in all things visible and invisible. There is a spiritual reality accessible to you at all times. Come to the present. Open yourself to this reality. Discover that the Spirit is a dimension of all of life.

Daniel, whose story I told earlier in this book, began his journey with the reading of Scripture. Night after night he stayed awake reading until he had made his way through the entire Bible. His thirst for knowledge was great indeed. But he didn't focus only on his private reading. In a few weeks he joined a small Bible-study group, he attended worship to hear the Word of God spoken from the pulpit, and he sought out people who could teach him. When I spoke with Daniel, I recognized ways in which he could become more like Christ, but I said nothing. I have confidence that the Spirit who awakened him will guide him in the way that he should go.

5. Let the light of Christ shine through you. He said, "I am the light of the world. Whoever follows me will never walk in darkness but will have the light of life" (John 8:12). But he who is the light of the world also said, "You are the light of the world" (Matt. 5:14). The critical distinction here is that the light that shines through us doesn't originate in us. Ours is a reflected light. This light not only illuminates our path; it shines upon the paths of others.

"Let your light shine," we read in Matthew 5:16. It's important to notice that this text doesn't say, "Shine your light." You don't have access to the switch; only Christ does. He must shine through you, and the joyful truth is that he does. You can't see this light with your own eyes, but others see it shining and reflect it back to you. Whether the people in your life are Christians or non-Christians, the light in you illumines their pathway. Your light warms their hearts and encourages them in the things of God. But remember that you yourself can't perform the miracle of the light. It is gift, it is grace, and it is from God.

Earlier in this book I told you the story of Kayron, a beautifully spiritual person. She struggled with the feeling that she was unworthy to serve God. The abuse that had created her sense of unworthiness was also the ground out of which her ministry grew. She persevered and developed a ministry to abused schoolchildren, helping pain-ridden little hearts unburden themselves of their deep secrets and their deep hurt. When she lamented her inability to speak with the children about Jesus, I reminded her that they saw him in her, even though they didn't know his name.

The same is true for you. The people upon whom your light shines see Jesus in you even if they don't know his name. And you needn't be perfect; remember that Jesus shines through the cracks in broken vessels. Praise Jesus for bringing the light, and let your light shine!

A Word to Congregations

Most of the comments that I've made in this book have been directed to individuals in the discernment process. In these closing pages I want to address congregations regarding their corporate call. I'm writing to a church that has begun to make the transition to a New Day, a church open to the moving of the Spirit and seeking to be faithful to a vision. The following suggestions should help such a church in this time of transition.

1. Nurture the presence of the Spirit among you through prayer and worship. Let a sense of wonder and awe permeate your gatherings. Listen for the call of God to you as a congregation.

2. Be patient with each other. Longtime traditionalists must be patient with those experiencing new life in the Spirit. Renewed individuals

should look to the traditional members with appreciation. Each needs the other. Newly awakened individuals bring energy and fresh life to the congregation, and the more traditional members serve to contain it and resist too rapid a change.

3. Focus on the future. Don't get mired down in the past, and don't become paralyzed with conflict in the present. Keep your eyes on the new possibilities that lie before you.

Dream big dreams.

Embrace impossible visions.

Keep hope alive.

Remember that you are the body of Christ, that Christ is alive in you, and that, with him, all things are possible.

An Exercise in Discernment

As an initial step, churches that are experiencing the new movement of the Spirit should establish a council for discernment. This council should be composed of the pastor, members of the governing body who represent both "old church" and "new church," and a few members from the congregation at large. The group should have from eight to twelve people in it.

Set a day and a time for the first meeting of the council. Ask all the participants to read this chapter beforehand. Invite all to be prayerful about the meeting.

The following timetable provides a fairly specific agenda for the council meeting. You can modify it to suit your needs, of course, but make sure that you make changes carefully, since a certain logic governs the agenda as it is given.

Meeting of the Council on Discernment

7:15 Call the council together and open with prayer. Explain that the aim of the council is to discern the way forward in the Spirit of Christ.

7:30 Have one person describe the ways in which the Spirit is at work in the congregation. Clearly state the issue about which you desire discernment.

8:00 Spend half an hour in silence in the presence of God.

8:30 Invite participants to share what came to them during the period of silence.

9:30 Give participants the opportunity to discuss the insights revealed, but make sure that everyone adheres to this rule: "Affirm an insight given before you raise an objection or a negative possibility." (Appoint one person to gently correct those who break this rule.)

10:00 Set a date for a second meeting of the council and dismiss the group.

Biblical Illustrations of God's Call

The community of faith in the New Testament, which we call "the church," was an assortment of individuals who had a profound awareness of the presence of the living God. God had manifested himself in Jesus of Nazareth, who lived among the people, showing them what the Creator God was like. Again and again various individuals gave witness to their experience of God through the person of Jesus. He became especially well-known to the disciples, who followed him, observed his ministry, and ate and drank with him in their homes. When he was crucified and raised from the dead, they continued to experience his presence with them: he guided them, called new disciples, and empowered all of them to continue his work.

While Jesus was with this community in the flesh, he promised to come back to them after his ascension. He fulfilled this promise on the Day of Pentecost, when he returned in the Spirit to inhabit this small community of followers. Now Christ not only transcended them but lived in them as an abiding presence. In and through this community he continued the ministry that he had begun during his historical existence.

Even a cursory reading of this community's story reveals the most obvious characteristic of their faith: an awareness of Christ in them and with them. Speaking with him seemed as natural as greeting a neighbor next door. Seeking his guidance and receiving new direction for the church's life happened so often that it became commonplace. One after another, members of this community were called by Christ to share in his ministry. These "called" individuals weren't ordained ministers in an institutional church as we know it today. They were simple, ordinary laypeople who encountered the risen Lord and were sent out on his mission.

I strongly believe that the church in the twenty-first century needs to pay attention to the Presence that birthed it and that has shielded it from extinction through the ages. I am persuaded that today we desperately need to heed the Presence in our hearts and in our midst. Neither the leadership nor the membership of congregations need to go elsewhere looking for Christ. Rather, we need to stop meaningless activity and empty busyness and give our full attention to Christ. Christ is calling, he is always calling, and we need to listen.

In the stories I told at the beginning of this book, I offered a few models of what happens when women and men listen for Christ's call. These stories are by no means exhaustive, but they are illustrative of Christ's renewed intention to call people into mission. Both individuals and the community as a whole need to be constantly alert for and receptive to the call of Christ. Indeed, Christ does call the community to act corporately in his mission.

The Anatomy of the Call of God

I not only want to make the claim that the early church experienced the immediate presence of the risen Jesus; I also want to walk into that world with you. I yearn for us today to breathe the air of the Presence they breathed and to feel the immediacy of the Presence they felt. Perhaps we can learn the language of the Spirit by listening with them. Hopefully an immersion in the Spirit of the New Testament community will inspire our imagination so that when we look at our present situation and the needs that cry out to us, we will be able to see with the eyes of Christ and listen with the ears of faithful disciples.

As we enter into this vital community of the Presence, what can we learn about the ways Christ called them to share in his ministry? What can we discover that will inform our listening for his call today? An examination of these various aspects of "call" will help us in our search for ways to discern more clearly the voice of God speaking to us.

The Story of a Call

If we could place ourselves in a gathering of the early church and ask them about Christ's call, what would they think of? Unquestionably, they would recollect Jesus' call to his first followers. They knew the story. They had heard it dozens of times from the lips of the fishermen and the tax collector.

If we asked a member of the community to tell us the story, he or she would say something like this: "One day Peter and Andrew were washing their nets by the Sea of Galilee when Jesus came by their docking point. The crowd following him was pressing in upon him, and he asked to use their boat. Peter agreed, and he rowed Jesus out a small way from the shore. From that point Jesus taught the crowd, but Peter listened to every word he said. When Jesus finished speaking, he told Peter to cast out his net. Peter was reluctant because he had fished all night and caught nothing. But he obeyed the Master, and he caught a huge number of fish — so many that he filled his boat and another boat to overflowing. In fact, the boats were so full that they began sinking. It was then that Peter fell down at Jesus' knees, confessing that he was a sinner. Jesus told him not to be afraid, that from now on he would be 'catching' people just as he had caught all those fish. And Peter believed and obeyed. He left everything to follow Jesus." (See Luke 5:1-11.)

What would the narrator be telling us about the way of Christ's call in this simple story, a story often repeated in the early church? If we strip away the skin of the narrative and look closely at the skeleton of the call, what do we discover? Don't we recognize that Jesus appears in Peter's world?

Initially Jesus invited Peter to take a very small step in associating with him: he asked Peter to lend him his boat. When he was seated in the boat on the sea, Jesus spoke to the crowd, but he was also aware that Peter was listening to him. By indirection Peter was learning what it means to be associated with Jesus. After he finished teaching, Jesus told Peter to fish in waters that Peter was certain had no fish. Although he had caught nothing the night before, Peter now filled the boat to overflowing with fish. In that moment the thin veil that shielded him from the transcendent world split, and he realized that Jesus was no ordinary man. When Peter's sinful humanness met Jesus' divine holiness, he cried out his feelings of helplessness. He fell on his knees at the feet of this extraordinary man, waiting for him to speak. As we can see, a series of events had prepared Peter to hear the call: his failure at his vocation, Jesus borrowing his boat, Jesus teaching the message, and Jesus directing and overseeing the catch of fish. That day Peter changed vocations — changed his life — because of his encounter with Jesus.

The Role of Memory in a Call

What is the role of memory in receiving or perceiving the call of Christ? Although Christ entered Peter's awareness that morning, it wasn't the first time that Peter had encountered Jesus. His brother Andrew, who was an associate of John the Baptist, had invited him to a meeting and conversation with Jesus before this fishing incident. Didn't Peter recollect that encounter when Jesus asked to borrow his boat? When Christ calls someone, the call often comes after a previous encounter, often one that the individual has stored away in memory for a long time.

In this imaginary encounter with people in the first-century church, I believe it would be enlightening to interview Saul of Tarsus, who became Paul. You recall his background. He was a Roman citizen born in Tarsus. He had traveled to Jerusalem to study the Jewish faith with Gamaliel, and he excelled among his peers. (See Acts 22:3.) He had been zealous in persecuting the church, and he was present at the stoning of Stephen, the first Christian martyr.

Saul of Tarsus was also the man who had a dramatic encounter with Christ on the road to Damascus. He was healed, baptized, and confirmed in his calling by a layman in Damascus named Ananias. Thereafter Saul preached the faith that he had once tried to destroy. His old colleagues sought to put him to death, but he was miraculously delivered. The leaders of the church in Jerusalem were suspicious of him until Barnabas, the good farmer from Cyprus, vouched for him. Saul (Paul) wrote to the Galatian church about this period in his life. He told them that after his introduction to the faith, he spent three years in Arabia. (See Galatians 1:13-17.) Clearly, Saul is the man for us to interview, and his sojourn in Arabia must be the subject of the conversation:

QUESTION: "Saul, tell us, if you will, what you did during those three years in Arabia."

ANSWER: "The major issue that consumed me during those three years was the meaning of the words spoken to me by Ananias after he baptized me. He told me what the Lord had said to him about me: 'Go, for he is an instrument whom I have chosen to bring my name before Gentiles and kings and before the people of Israel; I myself will show him how much he must suffer for the sake of my name' [Acts 9:15-16].

"At first I wondered what I had done to be chosen by Christ to be his instrument of communication to the Gentile nations, their kings, and my fellow Israelites. Frankly, I was overwhelmed. Although I had learned a great deal from Gamaliel, I still didn't know enough about Christ to be a spokesperson for him. But as I reviewed my life, I realized that I had been searching for the knowledge of God in all my studies in Jerusalem. And I had been shattered by the death of Stephen, who was a very good man. His radiant faith, even as he was dying, spoke like thunder in my ears.

"As I sorted out my childhood training, my study in Jerusalem, my experience on the road to Damascus, and Ananias's visit to me, it suddenly dawned on me that God had chosen me from my mother's womb [Gal. 1:15-16]. He had been working in my life all those years without my recognizing it. All the years that I thought I was seeking God, God was not only seeking me but was also using all of my experiences — even the negative ones — to equip me for the true task of my life.

"As I talk about those days I spent reflecting on my life, I'm still amazed at how close Christ was to me. He was so near that I spoke with him like I'm speaking with you now. At times he came so close that I felt I could touch him. The intimacy I had with him during those three years both shaped me and empowered me to endure the rejection, suffering, and pain that I would know in my service to him."

As the call to Saul illustrates, God calls us in the present, but often the material of the call is stored in our long memory. Everything in our lives has meaning, and it often takes years for it to become apparent. Nothing is ever wasted, not even our sin and misspent years.

Signs of the Presence in a Call

When anyone deals with a call, the primary question is, "How do I know this is God speaking to me?" Any person dealing with a call has not only the right but also the obligation to distinguish God's call from his or her own self-deception or secret longings. This question doesn't constitute a shockingly new discovery; it has always been a concern of the heart. In fact, this issue has been front and center for a long time.

At the dawn of the Christian era, John the Baptist confronted this issue both in himself and in the corporate concern of his followers. He was the forerunner of Jesus. John the Baptist's role was to identify and introduce Jesus to his followers and the masses of marginalized people who came to hear his message. When the day of introduction came, he was prepared with an answer to the question of whether or not Jesus was the Messiah.

One day when he was gathered with his disciples, John saw Jesus coming toward him. Immediately he exclaimed, "Here is the Lamb of God who takes away the sin of the world!" (John 1:29). How did he know this great truth? His disciples must also have wondered how he could make this affirmation so quickly.

John didn't hesitate to quell his own doubts as well as his followers' doubts. He did so by testifying to the sign he had gotten from God: "I saw the Spirit descending from heaven like a dove, and it remained on him. . . . The one who sent me to baptize with water said to me, 'He on whom you see the Spirit descend and remain is the one who baptizes with the Holy Spirit.' And I myself have seen and testified that this is the son of God" (John 1:32-34).

God's sign to John was the descending of the Spirit upon Jesus. John's sign to his disciples was his personal testimony. Through these events, which John didn't control, he was given a sign with which to identify Jesus. When he called Jesus the Son of God, he had confidence inspired by the symbol of the dove, and in making that pronouncement he fulfilled the call of God.

Similar signs manifested themselves to Peter when Jesus called him. The teaching that Peter heard while he was in the boat with Jesus was one of the signs. But the most convincing sign was the miraculous catch of fish. Indeed, catching a huge boatload of fish where there had been none just hours before, getting instructions for landing the fish from Jesus (a non-fisherman), and experiencing awe at this great spectacle — all of these were signs to Peter.

Saul was also given signs: the bright light that blinded him; the voice that spoke to him out of the light; the speaker, who identified himself as "Jesus, whom you are persecuting"; and the confirmation from Ananias that the same voice that spoke to Saul had also spoken to him.

The experiences of these New Testament disciples give us insight into the signs that help authenticate the call of God.

Typical Responses to God's Call

The call of God is generally a call to action. John the Baptist was called to introduce Jesus to his disciples and to Israel. Peter was called to become one of Jesus' associates in his ministry. Paul's call identified him as the Apostle to the Gentiles. Two other stories also illustrate how individuals in the early church era dealt with God's call. Their responses are not unlike our own, and therefore they are helpful for us to examine.

Ananias, a disciple of Jesus in Damascus, illustrates important aspects of responding to God's call. Perhaps he and others from Damascus were in Jerusalem on the Day of Pentecost. Maybe he was in the crowd who heard Peter's first proclamation of the gospel. Along with three thousand other Jews, he was baptized and instructed in the new faith.

After returning to Damascus, the group of believers gathered for prayer and worship. As Ananias was praying one morning, he had a vision, the kind that Teresa of Ávila would call an intellectual vision. In the vision he heard the Voice speak to him, and he answered properly, "Here I am, Lord." This response means "I'm listening." The Voice instructed him to go down to the street called Straight, find the hosue of Judas, and there look for a man named Saul, who was temporarily blind.

There was nothing fuzzy or confusing about this call. It was clear and specific, and Ananias heard it and understood it. But he was also frightened by it. Without hesitation he argued with the Lord. He explained to the Lord that he and his friends were a small, persecuted sect, and that the Jewish leaders in Jerusalem had sent Saul to investigate them. Ananias feared this man, who had the authority to apprehend Christians and take them back to Jerusalem and put them in jail. Ananias didn't say "No" to the Lord, but he put up strong resistance.

The Lord didn't rebuke or chasten Ananias for his resistance. (After all, Ananias had been honest with the Lord and had voiced legitimate concerns.) Instead, the Lord declared, "Go, for he is an instrument whom I have chosen to bring my name before Gentiles and kings and before the people of Israel; I myself will show him how much he must suffer for the sake of my name" (Acts 9:15-16). This response was enough for Ananias; it quelled his fears and empowered him.

Of all the experiences of calling in the New Testament, I think that I would most like to have been a part of this one. I would like to have been in Judas's house in Damascus on the street called Straight when Ananias came to minister to Saul. Think of it! Ananias — a layman, a recent convert to the faith, and a devout man of prayer — healing and ordaining a persecutor of the church who is to become the Apostle to the Gentiles.

His prayer for Saul expresses his complete embrace of the call: "Brother Saul, the Lord Jesus, who appeared to you on your way here, has sent me so that you may regain your sight and be filled with the Holy Spirit" (Acts 9:17). So fully did Ananias embrace the call of Christ that he forgot about Saul the persecutor and addressed him as "brother." He identified himself with Saul as one who also had been called. So this man who with integrity had wanted to reject the call found his way through his own resistance and did what the Lord asked. And as a consequence he baptized and commissioned the Great Apostle. (See Acts 9:10-20.)

Another response to God's call is illustrated by Mary, the mother of Jesus. When God called her, she was not so much in need of assurance of safety, as Ananias was; what she needed was more information. Her call was very confusing and seemingly impossible, and before answering it, she needed to have some issues clarified.

Although Mary had no preparation for or expectation of meeting the messenger of God, Gabriel appeared to her in Nazareth. Even though her worldview made room for heavenly beings, she was still frightened by the appearance of God's messenger. Realizing her fright, the angel calmed and comforted her with words of assurance: "Do not be afraid, Mary, for you have found favor with God" (Luke 1:30). As her fears subsided, the angel made this announcement: "You will conceive in your womb and bear a son, and you will name him Jesus. He will be great, and will be called the Son of the Most High" (Luke 1:31-32). How could this be, Mary inquired, since she was unmarried and still a virgin? Gabriel answered that the conception in her womb would be the work of God's Spirit.

With her questions answered and her fears quieted, Mary responded, "Here am I, the servant of the Lord; let it be with me according to your word" (Luke 1:38). This simple response of a young Jewish girl may be the purest expression of obedience in the entire New Testament. Her "yes" had tremendous implications. Pregnant without being married! At the time it was an invitation to scandal, especially if skeptics thought that she was claiming divine visitation to cover up an out-of-wedlock pregnancy. Yet she believed herself blessed above all women to carry in her womb and give birth to the Son of God. What simplicity! What utter obedience! "Let it be with me according to your word." (See Luke 1:26-38.)

As we reflect on these two responses to God's call, we can see that those who follow the biblical tradition do not go off half-cocked, following every whim or notion that comes to them. Rather, they resist immediate action, seeking information and getting their questions answered and their souls calmed before making important decisions. These are crucial insights for today's disciples.

The Role of Conversation in a Call

The call of God is personal, but it is neither private nor secretive. The one who is called must share the call to clarify it, shape it, and fully understand it. Once again, when we look to the New Testament for help in understanding how to deal with a call, we find numerous examples of sharing the sense of call with others through conversation.

Dialogue proved an important tool for Mary, the mother of Jesus. Shortly after Gabriel departed, Mary set out for the hill country of Judea to visit with her cousin Elizabeth, who was also pregnant. When she arrived at Elizabeth's home, Mary related the angel's message. In response, the fetus in Elizabeth's womb "leaped," and Elizabeth was filled with the Holy Spirit. In this state of ecstasy she said to Mary, "Blessed are you among women, and blessed is the fruit of your womb!" (Luke 1:42).

Mary answered with wonder and amazement in a song of praise: "My soul magnifies the Lord, and my spirit rejoices in God my Savior" (Luke 1:47). The record we have in the New Testament is stylized and formal, perhaps shaped through liturgical use. But I imagine that this record barely scratches the surface of the dialogue that went on between Mary and Elizabeth. Like Mary, Elizabeth had experienced a miraculous conception. She was well beyond her childbearing years, but the Lord had spoken to Zechariah, her husband, promising a son — and so the miracle had happened. Her son would not be the Son of God, the Messiah or Savior of the world, but he would be John the Baptist, who would prepare the way for Jesus. (See Luke 1:39-56.)

What did the dialogue with Elizabeth mean to Mary? As we can see, it was confirmation that she had heard Gabriel correctly. No doubt telling Elizabeth about her experience also clarified it in Mary's own mind. And knowing about Elizabeth's experience must have taken away some of the strangeness that Mary felt about her situation. Sharing their intimate experiences must have strengthened the bond between two special women. Like these two servants of God, persons in our day will also find confirmation and strength to fulfill their calls when they share them with trusted friends and relatives.

Like his mother before him, Jesus also knew the power of conversation. Before Jesus asked his disciples to be his followers, he spent time listening to them and answering their questions. For example, on the day that John the Baptist identified Jesus as the Lamb of God, several of John's disciples followed after Jesus. Jesus asked them about their intentions and then invited them to the place he was staying, where they spent the afternoon. Surely this was an afternoon of conversation about Jesus' person and his mission. (See John 1:35-42.)

Initially Jesus conversed with his disciples about his teaching to clarify their understanding. After a few months he formed the twelve into a small group for more intimate fellowship and conversation. He concluded his ministry by teaching them about his death and resurrection, when he gave them the symbols of bread and wine as a means to participate in his sacrifice. And these are but a few instances of the conversational style of Jesus' leadership. We wouldn't be far off the mark to conclude that his whole ministry was an extended conversation with his disciples in which he equipped them to carry on his ministry by helping them understand the nature and meaning of his call and theirs.

One other illustration will point to a different use of conversation. Paul often seems reluctant to engage in conversation. Frequently he's recounting what he already knows, or he's giving directions to members of congregations. If we return to his experience in Arabia, where his three years of seminary training took place, we get the impression that Jesus taught Paul what he needed to know to fulfill his calling. Sometimes Paul even boasts that he didn't confer with any other human being or engage the apostles in conversation but learned what he needed to know in Arabia.

When he returned from Arabia, he did go to Jerusalem, where he spent a few weeks conversing with Peter and his brother James. (See Galatians 1:13-24.) But this audience with the leaders in Jerusalem had to be brokered by Barnabas. It was Barnabas who vouched for Paul's integrity to Peter and James. Through his sponsorship, these leaders in the church opened themselves to conversation with Paul. It was a time to share the message each was preaching and a time for Paul to be confirmed by those men who had followed Jesus in the flesh. (See Acts 9:26-30.)

In dealing with a call, we need the help of other like-minded believers to help us discern and shape the call of God. How can this happen except through open and honest conversation?

The Transition between Calls

In one sense God's call is unchanging: God calls us to be in relation with Godself in everything intended for our lives throughout all our days. This permanent, persistent voice of the call does not vary. God is always calling us. But there are different contexts of God's call and thus different focuses of our vision and energy. God's continuous call helps us to make transitions from one form of call to another. Often our passion for one form must wane before a new form can be born.

Something like this happened in the life of Peter. We have examined the anatomy of his call: Jesus borrowed his boat, taught the people from it, directed the successful fishing expedition, and invited Peter to associate with him and his work. For about three years, Peter and the other trainees followed Jesus around Galilee, up to Caesarea Philippi, and finally up to Jerusalem. When they were in Jerusalem the last time before

Jesus' death, Peter recognized the hostility of the leaders, and he heard their threats. When someone asked him if he was one of Jesus' followers, he was afraid, and he denied that he even knew Jesus. No doubt Peter felt unsure about his calling at this point.

A friend of mine who was reflecting on the "time in between" calls described the pain of living in the darkness. During this time she had difficulty focusing on God's presence, on prayer, and on her future. She was afloat, but she felt like a boat without a rudder. "It was my darkest hour," she told me. Living between calls can be a period of great testing.

Peter was frightened by what he had experienced in Jerusalem. He lost the vision that had been growing in him since he had left his boat and his nets behind. So, not surprisingly, he went back to the thing that he knew best, seeking comfort in the familiar: fishing. But Jesus wasn't about to let Peter go. On the first Easter Sunday, Jesus sought Peter out — and the scenario of Peter's first call was played out again. Peter was out fishing with some of the other disciples, but hadn't caught anything. Just after daybreak Jesus appeared on the beach and called out to them, telling them to cast their net on the right side of the boat. Once again the net was filled to overflowing with fish — and at that point the disciples knew that the man on the shore must be Jesus. He prepared breakfast on the beach for Peter and his companions, and after the meal he talked with Peter alone, reconfirming Peter's call by telling him to "Feed my sheep." This conversation re-awakened Peter's sense of call, and his vision for the future was clarified through Jesus' new commission. (See John 21:1-19.)

Although it was brief — from Friday evening through Sunday morning of Passion Week — this was a "between-the-times" period for Peter. During those time he felt disillusioned with his old association and focus. But I believe this sense of disillusionment and detachment was necessary so that he could reaffirm his commitment to Jesus and hear him say, "Feed my sheep." The encounter with Jesus on the beach marked Peter's transition from Peter the disciple to Peter the apostle, a transition from following to leading.

Peter's "between the calls" period is a condensed version of the experience of everyone called by God. Answering God's call takes a certain shape when we first respond, but eventually that shape changes. Changes come about partly because of growth — because we change as our gifts develop more fully and God places us in roles of increasing responsibility. But growth is just one of many things that God may use to disengage us from one call and bring us to the new task we are to assume. The time between disengagement and re-engagement requires an extra measure of trust and sensitivity to the Spirit's work in our lives.

In this section I've outlined and explored various aspects of God's call in order to provide you with some parameters and dimensions of vocation. I hope that the bibilical explorations of call here will both awaken your call more deeply and bring it into sharper focus.

Bibliography

Farnham, Suzanne G.; Joseph P. Gill; R. Taylor McLean; and Susan M. Ward. *Listening Hearts: Discerning Call in Community.* Harrisburg, Pa.: Morehouse Publishing, 1991.

Friesen, Garry. *Decision Making and the Will of God.* Portland: Multnomah, 1980.

Hudnut, Robert K. *Call Waiting: How to Hear God Speak.* Downers Grove, Ill.: InterVarsity Press, 1999.

Johnson, Ben Campbell. *Discerning God's Will.* Louisville: Westminster/ John Knox Press, 1990.

————. *Listening for God: Spiritual Directives for Searching Christians.* Mahwah, N.J.: Paulist Press, 1997.

Kincaid, Ron. *Praying for Guidance: How to Discover God's Will.* Downers Grove, Ill.: InterVarsity Press, 1996.

Morris, Danny E., and Charles M. Olsen. *Discerning God's Will Together: A Spiritual Practice for the Church.* Nashville: Upper Room Books, 1997.

Palmer, Parker. *Let Your Life Speak: Listening for the Voice of Vocation.* San Francisco: Jossey-Bass, 2000.

Smith, Gordon T. *Courage and Calling: Embracing Your God-Given Potential.* Downers Grove, Ill.: InterVarsity Press, 1999.

Willard, Dallas. *In Search of Guidance: Developing a Conversational Relationship with God.* New York: HarperCollins, 1993.

Printed in the United States
126202LV00004B/6/A

9 780802 839619